You **can** *Write a* **Cookbook**

J. Kevin Wolfe

WRITER'S DIGEST BOOKS
CINCINNATI, OHIO
www.writersdigest.com

Visit our Web site at www.writersdigest.com for information on more resources for writers.

To receive a free weekly E-mail newsletter delivering tips and updates about writing and about Writer's Digest products, send an E-mail with "Subscribe Newsletter" in the body of the message to newsletter-request@writersdigest.com, or register directly at our Web site at www.writersdigest.com.

04   03   02   01   00   5   4   3   2   1

Library of Congress Cataloging-in-Publication Data

Wolfe, J. Kevin
   You can write a cookbook / by J. Kevin Wolfe
     p. cm.
   Includes bibliographical references and index.
   ISBN 0-89879-923-6 (pbk. : alk. paper)
    1. Food writing.

  TX644.W65   2000
  808'.066641—dc21   00-028990
                                                           CIP

Editor: David Borcherding
Cover designed by: Lisa Buchanan
Cover illustration by: Al Parrish
Production coordinator: Mark Griffin

ABOUT THE AUTHOR

 J. Kevin "Doc" Wolfe is the author of three cook-
books. As co-host of Everybody's Cooking, a ra-
dio food show on the X-Star Network, he has
interviewed the world's great chefs and cookbook authors, gaining great insights into cooking
and the trials of writing cookbooks. He regularly
lectures on cooking and consults companies on
food. With Chef Jimmy Gherardi he was instru-
mental in creating the "Chef'n Around" line of
cards for Gibson Greetings. Outside the food realm, his cartoons and
articles on creativity and humor have appeared in Writer's Digest Magazine. Riley Girt is his alter ego, who conducts the "US Senseless Survey"
and is heard on the nationally syndicated Gary Burbank Show. He is an
avid Net poet and writes copy for a nationally respected advertising firm.
He lives in Cincinnati with his wife and two sons.

TABLE OF CONTENTS

Release • Promotion Tips • Paid Advertising • The Promise of
the Big Interview • Mailing Lists • Media Savvy • Computer
Marketing • Free E-Mail • Using the Internet • Bookstore
Signings • Release Parties • Private Book Parties • Sales
Gimmicks • Free Recipes • Door-to-Door Flyers • Making the
Most of the Holidays • Supplementing Your Book Income

Is it possible that you'll read this book and write another *The Joy of Cooking*? Could you be jetting off to Paris to taste grapes for Möet, demonstrating how to soufflé on the *Today Show*, and then jogging over to Jersey to tape an arm-wrestling match with Martha Stewart for *Monday Nitro*?

Anything is possible.

Anyone with a good kitchen aptitude can write a cookbook. The American cookbook industry is looking for authors who can pen well-written, topic-focused cookbooks. Some publishers want practical, everyday-use cookbooks. Others are looking for cookbooks filled with gorgeous photos and meant to sit on every coffee table in America. These publishers look for self-promoting authors who are charismatic and can demonstrate their skills with flair in front of crowds and cameras. If this is you, read on and we'll see you on *Nitro* with Martha begging for your mercy.

On the other hand, if you simply want to write a cookbook as a fundraising venture for your favorite charity, this book gives you the step-by-step procedures to write it, promote it, and sell more copies than you ever thought possible.

For the person who's creative in the kitchen, this book shows you not only how to write your cookbook, but how to make it a success and turn your cooking into a career.

And if you just want to write a cookbook as a family keepsake, you'll find out how to turn those recipes and memories into something that will be treasured for years to come.

All you really need to write a cookbook is the ability to make a tasty dish. That's all. While many cookbooks written by famous chefs sell well and any cookbook benefits from its author having professional training, it's not required. Many successful cookbook authors are a combination of good home cooks, bold experimenters and good writers.

THE STATE OF THE KITCHEN/THE STATE OF THE COOKBOOK
In the 1950s, the kitchen was firmly guarded ground. Mom, Grandma, or a housekeeper was there for hours a day, cooking. You could taste the love and toil in every bite of that massive, dripping roast or that delicate chocolate cake.

In those days the kitchen was off-limits to men. We all ate in the dining room, and dinner was served promptly at 5:30.

Then the decline of the kitchen set in, and we were happy to let it happen, in the name of "convenience." Electric stoves started popping up. Mr. Swanson saw an opportunity, and the turkey and mashed potato TV dinner was invented.

People forgot the sacred secrets, like how to dissolve yeast—the veritable "Big Bang" of home baking. Mom found herself getting a job with those extra hours to help pay for all this "convenience." Six o'clock rolled around, and the kitchen was dark and cold.

We suddenly realized we had lost our culinary roots. The vision of Grandma slaving in the kitchen became an almost holy sight in our minds. The secrets of her perfect pie dough died with her. We've become far removed from that way of life, and now we want it back.

In the 1950s, when cooking was a two- or three-meal-a-day endeavor, the household had "a" cookbook. The cookbook library when I was growing up fit in a drawer with the dried beans. By the 1990s we sought that lost knowledge of the kitchen. And sixty years after its first self-published release, *The Joy of Cooking* was once again updated and re-released. It sold a million copies instantly.

With prominent Chef Jimmy Gherardi, I host a radio cooking show on a public network called "Everybody's Cooking." We interview the world's top cookbook authors every week which gives me a good overview of the industry. I see two opposite trends right now: People who never had a cooking "bible" are seeking one. And people who cook once a week are spending an entire weekend day cooking one meal for friends and family. They make a huge deal out of it. The recipes are from an expensive cookbook that sits on their coffee table the other six days. While one group wants to get back to basics, learn good nutrition, and get Mom back in the kitchen, the other group fantasizes all week about an exotic meal that they can only cook on Sunday. They work harder to buy more cookbooks to dream about cooking. They're armchair chefs.

The cookbooks for this melting pot of ours have never been hotter. People who learned how to cook Thai last year are cooking "New Thai" now. We learned to cook true ethnic, now we're learning to cook ethnic that's been tempered with the latest fads. Food trends are changing quickly. Some people want to cook a "Yankee Pot Roast with French Herbs and a Mild Korean Dark Sauce," while some want to know how to cook a plain old pot roast like Mom did. Bold experiments and comfort food are what people want.

Many bookstores are disappearing while the surviving bookstores are growing larger. The size of the cookbook section is increasing, filled with books on every ethnic style and health concern in existence. And many cookbooks are read by people who only fantasize about cooking

Celebrity chefs used to be few. Julia Child, Graham Kerr and James Beard were about the only names you could think of thirty years ago. Now there are hundreds of chefs and cookbook authors getting visibility in all mediums. PBS is deluged with cooking shows, and there's the twenty-four-hour-a-day cable Food Network. It seems that even those who don't cook love to absorb the information and become chefs by osmosis.

The good news is there's plenty of room for new cookbook authors. Megachef, cooking show host, food columnist and culinary futurist cookbook authors all have found a niche.

So here we are in the new millennium. What's cooking for the next thousand years? At the start of the last one, they had just thought up the concept of pizza, and a thousand years later we're still arguing if it gets anchovies or not.

1 WHY WRITE A COOKBOOK?

Cookbook writing is destiny.

I know that many great novelists would turn their nose up at that idea, but those of us with a passion for cooking know that our cookbooks are more than just collections of recipes. They're epics we toiled over and they can be recreated in any kitchen in America.

You might want to write a cookbook and print up ten copies as gifts for your family. You may want to organize a cookbook that will sell two hundred copies as a church or PTA fundraiser. Or you may want to become the next Martha Stewart or Emeril Lagasse with a million copies in print. And if you are just writing a cookbook to give to your family, we all know what's in the back of your mind: you're hoping MegaTitle Publishers will call and say they want to run off a million copies or two.

Whatever your reason, if you want your cookbook to be read, and more importantly, if you want your cookbook to be used, you need to realize that a cookbook is more than just the binding that holds a few recipes together. It requires just as much thought as the great American novel. The only difference is with the great American novel, you don't get to sample the food.

THE PURPOSE OF A COOKBOOK

If the purpose of your cookbook is only to bring good recipes to people, you'd better think deeper. Most successful cookbooks have a theme that bonds the recipes. Even a staple cookbook like *The Joy of Cooking* has an almost biblical theme of being the last word on cooking. Almost any recipe imaginable is there.

Since your cookbook will probably contain between fifty and two hundred recipes, it's best to focus your recipes on a course or meal (appetizers, lunch, etc.), on a style of cooking (wraps, Peruvian, etc.), or on a specific

4

topic (football game watching food, brunch, dryer vent bamboo steaming).

Even if you just intend for family members to get a copy of your cookbook, it needs a story to bind the recipes together. It needs a treatment that makes those recipes more than just lists of ingredients and instructions.

You may be truly shocked to find that a vast number of people read cookbooks, but never cook from them. The public demands well-written cookbooks and they want flavor in the writing as well as the recipes. Decide what slant you want your book to have and go from there.

TYPES OF COOKBOOKS

There are four basic types of cookbooks:

The Biographical/Autobiographical Cookbook

The Historical Cookbook

The Collaborative Cookbook

The Best-Seller Cookbook

The Biographical/Autobiographical Cookbook

If you are writing a cookbook that you will give to a few family members, you can make the "lead character" a person (or group of people) from your family. It could be you, or it could be your spouse, children, ancestors or other relatives. You can even write an autobiography that goes alongside your recipes. Tell how the recipe came about. Is there an interesting story about what happened once when you served the recipe? People know you because of your good food, now tell them about yourself.

These books are usually written for the family but can end up on an editor's desk at a publishing company. Treat this book like it is your memoir, because it is. A hundred years from now when the photos have faded and the letters have been lost, your cookbook will still be sitting on a shelf in your great-great-great-grandchildren's home. If the book is about you it may be the one surviving testament of your existence. Write what you want future generations to know about you, your family and your food.

Here are some suggestions:

Pick a focal point. The most logical center of attention is you, but some people feel self-conscious and would rather write about someone else. If you feel this way, you're better off to turn the focus toward another family member or a group of people (sisters, etc.). Here are some possible topics:

- **Mom.** Most likely she taught you to cook and provided some of your recipes. There may be wonderful stories associated with them.
- **Dad's eating habits.** Even if he didn't cook, how he controlled the dinner table tells a lot about your influences growing up. I have friends with wonderful stories of how their dad was a totalitarian at dinner. One evening he demanded that two giggling sisters not make a sound through the rest of dinner. They continued to giggle, however, and after a few minutes of his stern-facing them, one quietly raised her hand and informed him that his tie was in his soup.
- **Grandma.** She is a logical choice if you spent a lot of time in her kitchen. Grandma may have had a lot of philosophical advice or been the family psychiatrist. Her sayings can be woven into the book.
- **Cousins.** Collect recipes from your cousins and put them into stories alongside your own recipes. Tell about the times you were together.
- **Neighbors.** Did a neighbor's cooking influence you? This is a great topic. Ask the neighbor or family for recipes and other background information you may have never known.
- **Cooking at a summer place.** How did the family cook in this different environment? Did you eat what was fresh and local in the summer time? Visit the place again to refresh memories.
- **Your immediate family.** Recalling memories and the recipes associated with them can be therapeutic for all. Recipes can be tied in with stories about your spouse or your children or tales of your childhood.
- **Your heritage.** Whether you come from Italy and live in New Hampshire or came to Sacramento from Tallahassee, your environment influenced your cooking. If you moved around a lot, each place can become a chapter.

Kitchens provided each of us with a different experience growing up. What made yours unique?

Touching and humorous character portraits of family members are a joy to read by those who know them. Outsiders also enjoy peeking into the windows of your life if you make the people real and entertain them with vibrant descriptions and anecdotes.

Give each recipe a story. If it's a Sunday cake, tell what happened on

Sundays in your house. A pithy one-page tale before each recipe will make that recipe special. Draw a picture in the reader's mind that will live like it does in your memory.

The Historical Cookbook

Historians are now using old cookbooks as great resource material. It sounds far-fetched, but years ago cookbooks and the Bible were about the only reading material in the house. Recipes have been found in hieroglyphics, but the oldest known cookbook titles date back to Greece in 400 B.C. The first prominent American cookbooks were written mostly by women in the 1820s. Some authors, like Mrs. Horace Mann, used their cookbooks to express their temperance views.

Check the margins of cookbooks that have been in your family for years. You may find a note that Grandma used your favorite cake recipe for a wedding many years ago. Or you may find that a cousin used a roast recipe for bear meat during a long winter.

Your cookbook can be written to preserve history through the recipes and tales of your immediate family. You can even dig into the culinary techniques of your ancestors with the memories old recipes revive. Usually historical books are written for extended family, but they may be marketable to others. Author David Warda wrote a cookbook that included family memories and snapshots. The idea became salable when he wrapped around those memories and keepsakes the story of his Assyrian ancestry. So *Assyrian Cooking* hit the market.

Research for this type of cookbook is simple. Have a family reunion and ask everyone to cook the oldest family recipe they know. You can fill hours of audio and video recordings with tales of family meals.

Get your hands on the original of every recipe you can. Any margin notes in the cookbook probably weren't included when the recipe was copied by hand, so you may be missing out on some history. However, paper was expensive years ago; no telling what the original recipe was written on. It may be on the back of a voided land deed. If the recipe was clipped from a newspaper, look for a date or events in the stories next to the recipe that might help you date it.

You might snoop through old copies of the local cooking column in the town paper at the library and find a favorite recipe from childhood came from there. Census information can help answer riddles. You might wonder why all of Great-Grandma's recipes served twelve when she had a family of three. Census data may show that nine relatives were living in the house during a war or during hard times.

Historical cookbooks can also be about a topic unrelated to you. Books on Colonial cooking, Shaker cooking, or cooking from other periods in U.S. history can sell well in small runs. These books, printed by small publishers and self-publishers, sell well at vacation spots in most any part of the nation. A lot of historical periods are not oversaturated with books. There are not that many Civil War, Great War, Pilgrim, Native American or Dust Bowl cookbooks, just to name a few. If you have researched an era, or are fascinated by cooking of an era, you've got the start of a cookbook.

The Collaborative Cookbook

Collaborative cookbooks are usually compiled by school, church or social groups as fundraisers. These books are not limited to a small audience, like the parents of students. With an appealing title and theme they can sell well in bookstores too.

The book should tell about its cause even if it has a different theme. If it's the *Mennonite Heights Community Church Fiesta Cookbook* you can offset the Tex-Mex recipes with sidebars about the church. Tell about the church, the church's food events, and the cooks who worship there. Even people who don't contribute recipes can contribute humorous stories about events that have happened at the church. Maybe the church has done a fiesta night for years and there are great stories about what happened those nights or while the dishes were being prepared in the kitchen.

If the book is a school fundraiser, let people know about the school and its history. Did someone famous go to school there? They might be overjoyed to write a foreword. Are there funny PTA or band stories? Does the sports team have a great history? Tell about teacher's experiences and memories of the school. If the cookbook is well written it will appeal to the general reader and not just to football parents.

If the book is for a social group, what does the group do? How has the group helped the community? What will the proceeds of the book go to? Don't just make a list of past group presidents, give a concise, well-written history of each of them. Portray them as a person with a story and not just a name and date. The more human the book is the more it will be read and cherished.

8

Most likely there is a great deal of pride in the projects the book proceeds will benefit. That pride should be reflected in the cookbook. If people are drawn in by the cause, they may buy more books.

You must be careful if the book is to benefit a somber subject like a medical charity or a tragedy. Be tactful and tasteful in your writing. If the book benefits a medical cause, don't turn stomachs:

- Don't talk in depth about an illness or tragedy. This is very unappetizing. Cookbooks should not make people sick.
- Don't dwell on someone's death. Talk about memories of life rather than how a person died from a painful illness.
- Don't keep saying what a good cause it is. Prove it's a good cause by writing touching stories about how the money will be used and especially what it was used for in the past.
- Don't overly thank everyone throughout the book. There is room for thank-you's at the start of the book. That's where they belong.
- Don't dwell on the negative. People want to hear stories of hope. They want to know about the successes and progress.

If the group has had previous cookbooks, you can probably track down copies and do a historical book of the best recipes from past eras. These compilation cookbooks are easy to do and usually have a lot of appeal. Of course, the last chapter should be current recipes. There are always those in a group that can be adamant about getting their recipes in print. These people usually buy a lot of cookbooks, too, so current recipes in this type of project keep the peace *and* sell books.

The Best-Seller Cookbook

This is the toughest type of cookbook to write. It's what everyone hopes their book turns into. It is very important that you have a theme for the book or you may as well give up now. The best-seller has to capture the world's attention, and then its heart, to succeed. It must appeal to the masses or at least to a very specific audience to make it.

More cookbooks are being published today than ever before and people are paying more for them. Fifty-dollar cookbooks are now commonplace on America's coffee tables. The bad news is that some cookbooks have gotten gimmicky, with little substance and lousy recipes. *The Left Handed Plumber's Cookbook* may grab the attention of a publisher; just make sure the recipes are good enough to make the book useful and not just a novelty read.

The good news is that there is plenty of room for great cookbooks, provided they have solid themes. My first cookbook, *The Fat-Free Junk Food Cookbook,* was accused of the heinous crime of gimmickry. But it was the first fat-free cookbook listed in *Books In Print* and many other fat-free books have since followed. If you start a trend, you're exonerated from gimmick prosecution. Of course, I'm still on parole from the Trendy Police.

I had plenty of fantastic recipes and could have written a failed cookbook at anytime in my life, but I found a fat-free need in the market and no books there to fill it. I published my first cookbook myself and sold thirteen thousand copies. That got the notice of a big publisher who picked it up. Being in the right place at the right time is everything.

2 THE INGREDIENTS OF A GOOD COOKBOOK

There are certain basic elements in most best-selling cookbooks. Use them no matter what type of cookbook you're writing and your chances of success will rise dramatically. These elements are:

A valid reason for writing it

A high mouthwatering factor

Simple instructions

Logical chapters

A foolproof index

Tasty results (that will make readers open the book again)

Solid writing

An appealing visual aspect

A VALID REASON FOR WRITING IT

The days of throwing some good recipes together and making a successful cookbook are gone. If you're planning to sell your book, check out the market. What's hot now (wraps, smoothies and low-sugar recipes) may not be hot by the time your book is printed. Read the culinary magazines. Check food trends on the Web. Figure out what's going to be hot next year and you can make a career of writing cookbooks.

To write a book that will sell well, there must be a need for your cookbook; you've got to fill a void. If you are the first to discover the void, you may have to cite evidence that it exists in order to get a publisher interested. Book editors are always looking for new topics and novel approaches to older topics.

Steven Raichlen went to Workman Publishers with the idea of a grill cookbook. As the book took shape, publisher Peter Workman realized the potential scope of the book. Steve wound up in twenty-nine countries doing research on grilling and barbecue. (He says the best barbecue he may have had was grilled in a hubcap in Vietnam.) He turned in a two-thousand page manuscript that was edited into *The Barbecue Bible*. It became a hot seller in a year that saw a huge number of grill-oriented cookbooks.

Madhur Jaffrey is an actress who likes to cook. She first wrote at a time when America was starting to take a liking to Indian food. Her original idea of an Indian cookbook has spawned a series of Indian-influenced cookbooks. Her books are good reading, with mouth-watering, informative introductions that are sometimes longer than the recipes. Since she also has skills in front of the camera, she was a natural for doing two public television series on Indian and Far East cooking. A new edition of her classic, *An Invitation to Indian Cooking*, has been released twenty-four years later.

Ed Espe Brown was the cook at the Tassajara Zen retreat in the California mountains. His *Tassajara Bread Book* is a Zen testament to practical bread baking. In 1970, there were few "health food" cookbooks on the market. Baking bread had become a lost art, and Ed's book presented the chore as therapy. The simple basic recipes in the little brown book led the *Washington Post* to call it "the bible of bread making." It led to two more books in the series and a commercial bakery in San Francisco. More small health-conscious bakeries started popping up. Big chains opened bakeries across America based on the idea.

These three people came up with the right theme for their cookbooks at the right time. You need to do the same to establish a valid reason for writing your cookbook.

THE MOUTHWATERING FACTOR

A very important element of any cookbook is the mouthwatering factor. People can't taste a recipe until they prepare it, so you've got to make their mouths water with its description. A color photo or a drawing helps even more.

Do you have a favorite cookbook? If it doesn't have photos, there is a good chance it has some recipe descriptions that make you drool like one of Pavlov's dogs.

We remember smells and tastes very well. If you can revive those memories in a description of the smell of a classic cake baking and the taste of it hot from the oven, people will want to try the recipe or maybe even buy the book.

Involve all the senses. If someone accuses your recipes of being erotic, you're probably on the right path.

SIMPLE INSTRUCTIONS

Easy, readable instructions are important. This doesn't mean you can't use a few complex recipes; it just means that they must be laid out in easy-to-follow steps.

Recipes are not rocket science, but some cookbook authors treat them as such. The most frustrating thing to a cook is an unclear, complex recipe that is murky at a critical step. Simply written, readable recipes are a must for a successful book. Great cooks are not offended by easy, simple recipes; they're offended if you don't take the time to lay out the process in simple procedures.

LOGICAL CHAPTERS

There's nothing worse than a cookbook that has no order to the recipes. The order can be as simple as "Appetizers, Entrées, Desserts." Logical grouping of the recipes also adds to the mouthwatering factor. For example, an ice cream recipe, followed by a steak recipe, followed by a cinnamon roll recipe is not an appetizing order.

Though your recipe box may be haphazard, you will probably need to organize similar recipes into chapters. Order your chapters in a way that makes sense. If you treat your chapters with the same care that a novelist does, your book will seem like a book, and not a bundle of recipes.

A FOOLPROOF INDEX

The most usable cookbook is one with a comprehensive index. Make your recipes easy to find and the book is less likely to sit on a shelf. The index should include every possible listing for a recipe. For example, Chocolate Orange Bundt Cake should be listed as:

Bundt Cake, Chocolate Orange
Cake, Chocolate Orange Bundt
Chocolate Orange Bundt Cake
Orange Bundt Cake, Chocolate

People want immediate access to your recipes and a thorough index is the only way they can find them fast. Think about it: when you grab a cookbook to find a recipe, do you go to the table of contents, which only gives you a general idea where the recipe is in the book, or do you go straight for the index and find the specific page number? The back of a cookbook is used much more than the front.

TASTY RESULTS

The first recipe someone tries better be good or the cookbook will never be opened again. Be sure to use only recipes that taste good and work well every time in any kitchen.

Your lips and other parts of your mouth contain a few taste buds, but it's the tongue that is the chief justice as far as flavors are concerned. Your tongue also is very sensitive to texture and temperature. Generally you taste salty, sweet, and sour flavors with the tip and outer edge of your tongue and bitter flavors with the back of your tongue. Recently it has been discovered that some people are "supertasters" with more taste buds than normal. Your sense of smell, it should be noted, also greatly influences the taste of things. Without it foods taste bland.

What does your tongue like? Is it the typical American tongue? Do some "taste tests." Try a regular soft drink next to a diet soft drink. Close your eyes. Can you taste a difference? Try a flat and a carbonated soft drink. One causes the sensation of bubbles on your tongue and the other doesn't. Do they taste different because of this? Try a cheap cake mix and a home-made cake. Can you taste the chemicals and preservatives in one? When you consciously test, it's surprising how sensitive your palate is.

I have heard some cookbook authors talk in great detail about how they formulated a recipe. They speak of fooling the tongue to believe that there's fat in a recipe by thinly coating a roll with butter and salt so the initial flavor sensation is perceived throughout the food. They work on eliminating aftertaste almost as much as improving the flavor. Such dedication to detail can only improve your book.

Be willing to tamper with the flavor of your recipes. Will the cake benefit from an extra teaspoon of vanilla? Or if you cut the vanilla to half a teaspoon do some of the more subtle delicate flavors in the cake start to come forward? Work and rework your recipe to make your results as tasty as possible. Bold flavors are hot right now, but you can be assured there will be a subtle flavor backlash too.

14

And by all means experiment with new flavors. There are unusual flavor combinations that need to be appreciated. For instance, I co-wrote a kid's cookbook with my four-year-old son. One of our recipes was fried-banana-lime-spinach made with brown sugar. It sounds disgusting, but has a wonderful flavor that even gets kids to try spinach.

When I was young my mom once made an apple pie while she had a cold which was dubbed "Mongolian Fire Pie." The cayenne powder jar and the cinnamon jar looked identical, as did the contents. Without the aid of smell, the two were easy to confuse, so a tablespoon of cayenne went into the filling. The wonderful-looking pie had quite a kick. My dad and I, both being fans of hot food, loved it.

Be bold and try new combinations. Generally, you would put only a few experimental successes in a cookbook, but you may even find your own niche and become famous for your wild, wonderful combinations and experimental cooking techniques. Bob Bloomer, The Surreal Gourmet, is always asked to prepare his dishwasher fish recipe on TV—a whole fish wrapped in foil and cooked in the dishwasher. (He recommends lemon detergent for a little touch of citrus flavor.) A whole book of such unique recipes can do well if presented right.

SOLID WRITING

The writing that accompanies your recipes must be first-rate. Some authors say they write cookbooks because they can't write anything else. Tie that idea to a railroad track and snicker while it gets run over. You have very little space in a cookbook for recipe introductions and sidebars, so you've got to use words effectively. The great cookbook writers are all just plain great writers.

One of the most useful books on writing is George Mair's *How to Write Better in One Hour*. This out-of-print book lives up to its pretentious title. You may find it at the library or in a secondhand bookshop. Learning the basics and reviewing them is helpful to every writer before clicking a pen to paper.

People expect good recipes; it's the notes and tips that go with them that ensure the book will be used over and over again. There should be something of yourself in your recipes. Do people tell you you're a good teacher? Include informative tips as notes and sidebars. Thanks or no thanks to *USA Today*, America expects that little extra anecdote on the side or at the bottom of the page. Do people say you tell great stories? Insert the best ones where appropriate, but keep them concise. Are you told you have a sense of humor? Work it into your recipes. Pass the recipes around to friends and keep the anecdotes that make them smile or laugh.

Be critical of what you include. Always ask yourself if it truly informs or entertains. If it doesn't, take it out.

AN APPEALING VISUAL ASPECT

A cookbook should be laid out so it is readable and not visually confusing. Illustrations and photos can make instructions clear, as well as show what a dish should look like when finished. The greatest shock to a cookbook author is when someone else tries to make your recipe and the result is nothing like yours. Any recipe that relies on good presentation will benefit from an illustration or photo. Simple, well-done line drawings also can be very enticing as well as instructional.

Color photos are the most appealing visual element, but are cost-prohibitive, even with large publishers. Color plays a big part in the appeal of food; black-and-white photos are not usually appealing. While it's true that Edward Weston shot some beautiful erotic black-and-white masterpieces of peppers and other vegetables, the truth is they are sensual but not appetizing. Our eyes are so trained for color today that old black-and-white photos of food that once were considered appealing, now seem unappetizing.

You're better off with classy line drawings. Examine *Cooks Illustrated Magazine* and you'll see just how effective line drawings can be. Food illustrations need to look like the food. If a cake illustration looks more like a slice of peppered bread than it does a slice of pound cake, it will not make the recipe more enticing.

If you're working with an artist, tell him if you're not satisfied with the illustration. An onion needs to look like an onion and not a rotten orange. Be specific. Tell him what bothers you about the drawing. The more exact you are about the problem, the easier it is for him to correct it.

3 HOW TO WRITE A RECIPE

Don't think a recipe can be a passionate piece of writing? A well-written cookbook can be more passionate than love poetry. Examine the work of a mystery writer whose characters routinely speak with a passion about food. Delectable food talk heightens the senses.

For many people, eating food is the most sensuous thing they do. It's one of the few things we do in life that involves all of our senses. You see the rich color of food coming out of the oven. The movement of the steam wafting up gives you a sensation of heat. You hear the food bubble. The distinct warm scent of the food pervades your nose. You feel the distinctive texture as it touches your tongue. You taste the delicacy. You let out a satisfied "Mmmmmm."

The mouthwatering factor is what makes your recipes irresistible. Use passion in your writing to create it. The greatest compliment is when a reader tells you how good one of your recipes is and you then learn that she's never made it. If she's only experienced it through your description and could taste it in words, you're baking your recipes in the oven of their mind.

THE TITLE

The title is the first contact someone has with your recipe. You need to make sure it's not the last. If all that precedes the recipe is the title "Fudge," what's the incentive to try it? There are a million fudge recipes. Describe the result of their labors. "Chocolate Peanut Butter Meltaway Fudge" tells you what it tastes like. It tells you what it does in your mouth. It draws an appetizing picture.

If the title is lame, no one will bite. One of the most popular recipes in my cookbooks is "Chocolate Therapy Cake." Many have tried it because the name caught their eye and their tastebuds. It is descriptive, but not too pretentious. It gives a description of what the cake does for your palate and also a suggested use. Well-chosen words can say a lot. The title will be best if it's two to five words long. Beyond seven words and you've lost the reader unless you use some kind of phrase. "Gandhi's Died-And-Gone-To-Nirvana Lemon Cake" has a ring to it. Be especially descriptive of the recipes you're really proud of. These are the ones you'll want to be known for.

Don't try to cram too much into a title. "Massive Blueberry Dream English Scones" is cumbersome. "Blueberry Dream Scones" pretty much says it all and is much more clear.

Don't try to get too many ingredients into the title. "Collard, Kale, and Mustard Greens in a Fresh Green Lime Vinaigrette" is more than can be swallowed. "Tangy Lime Greens" clearly gets the recipe's outcome across.

Some of the cooks who win cook-offs and bake-offs swear by long titles. They say the longer and more descriptive the title, the better your chance of winning a ribbon. Generally for cookbooks, however, a few descriptive, powerful words work best. Marcel Desaulniers' *Death By Chocolate* has become a national catch phrase. My "Scorned Woman Hot Sauce" owes much of its popularity to its clever name.

Some of my other successful titles have been: "Wicked Cinnamon Rolls," "Anti-Gravity Biscuits," "Egg Beaters Foo Yung," "I Swear They're Fat-Free French Fries," "Broccoli Incognito," "Sweet Heat Barbecue Sauce," "Seasoning Assault," " 'They Sure Don't Taste Like' Vegeburgers," and (the obligatory Elvis recipe) " 'Nana Pudding Fit for the King."

Advertising agencies use "flavor words" in their food advertising and food packaging. These can be worked into titles to contribute to the mouthwatering factor. Flavor words sound like what they mean. The word "fresh" sounds like a head of lettuce being broken open. "Crisp" sounds like a cracker cracking. "Crunch" sounds like a tortilla chip being bitten. "Chocolatey" sounds like teeth sinking into soft candy. These adjectives all imply some kind of action the senses can relate to. Say the following list of words out loud, slowly and with feeling. Your mouth should be watering before you're finished.

bubbly
charred
cracked

crackling
creamy
fizzy
golden
gooey
grilled
oozing
rich
seared
sizzling
stinging
sweet
tangy
tantalizing
tender
zesty
zingy
zippy

Use only one flavor word per recipe and make sure it enhances the food it's describing. "Crunchy Green Beans" doesn't draw a good picture. Neither does "Tangy Chocolate" or "Tender Pork Rinds." There are those cookbook authors who may not want their recipes to sound like descriptions on a TV commercial. If that's you, then consider this a list of words to avoid.

A word of caution: Don't get carried away with empty superlatives in your titles. The recipe must be able to deliver what the title promises. "Never Fail . . ." means that even if a three-year-old fixes it, it better not fail. "World's Greatest . . . ," "Best Ever . . . ," ". . . Worthy of a Messiah" type titles should be used sparingly. Close scrutiny always follows pretense.

THE DESCRIPTION

Once readers see your title, you've probably only piqued their curiosity. Now you have to get them to try the recipe. It's best to start each recipe with an opening paragraph. This should tell them the selling points of the recipe, entertain them and (most importantly) entice them.

Describe the end result of the recipe. "This is a dense cake" doesn't have the same ring to it as "This moist, dense cake takes you back to Grandma's house on Sundays." Draw vivid pictures that make the mouth water. Are your cookies soft or crunchy? Let the readers know. Is the dish impressive looking with such a memorable flavor that it's suitable for serving the boss at dinner? Can you relate the outcome of the recipe to something they know? For instance, does the coffee cake topping resemble a streusel topped pie? They will want to hear about it.

Point out the advantages of the recipe. Is it quick and easy? Is it better the second day? Does it freeze well either before or after baking? Does it make a good leftover. Does it smell so good it makes the neighbors drop by? Then say so.

The opening paragraph is the place to drop in a quick tale about the history of the recipe. Ed Espe Brown's "Top of the Wall Cookies" recipe title in the *Tassajara Bread Book* intrigued me enough to read the first paragraph. So do you want to know what it means? The recipe was created the day they finished making the top of the kitchen wall at the Zen monastery.

My Aunt Carolyn makes a cake I've dubbed her "Public Servant Cake." When people try it, I tell them the story of how it got its name. Periodically Aunt Carolyn takes the cake down to the police station and in her charming Southern accent says, "I just thought I'd show my appreciation for the hard work you officers do. By the way, I'm going on vacation next week. You think you could drive by the house a time or two and check up on the place?" The neighbors say the police stop by and check the locks four or five times a day while she's gone. Whenever she has something like a couch that the garbage men aren't suppose to take, she appears at the curb with her cake and both the cake and the couch are gone. That kind of story will not only make your book a hit with family, but with the public as well. By the way, the real name of the cake is a little more descriptive of why it's so popular: "Apricot Nectar Cake."

If there's a story about the recipe, tell it. If this is the meatloaf recipe you had to make because Ed shot his foot and didn't bag the deer for dinner, work the story in. And if you're writing a group cookbook, have everybody write a few words about each recipe and include the best anecdotes in the book. Somebody else may have a great story about a recipe that you never knew about. A little storytelling skill can bring a recipe to life.

Here are some examples of descriptions from my books:

For Cream of Carrot Soup:

> "This bright orange soup is surprisingly hearty. The white wine gives it a classy flavor. It's fine enough to serve to visiting dignitaries . . . or people you want to treat as such."

It's short, but tells you that the soup is colorful and filling. It tells you what it tastes like and that it's suitable for guests.

For Stew Beans:

> "The concept of stew beans probably comes from hard times. During the Depression and the war, there was little meat for cooking. But folks still had stew, with beans taking the place of beef. Pintos are used in this recipe since they have a beefy ambiance. The thick gravy created by the starch in the potatoes makes the meal hearty enough to pour over cornbread (page 82)."

It gives a little history about how the dish came about and lets you know the dish looks a lot like beef stew. It tells you how thick it is and gives you a serving suggestion.

For Balsamic Honey Dressing:

> "Herbed balsamic vinegar is the most flavorful of all vinegars. It's so potent, only small amounts are used. In Modena, the Italian town the vinegar comes from, it's rumored that garage mechanics use it to charge ailing car batteries. (But that's just a rumor.)
>
> "This simple recipe uses lots of honey to tame the acids and coax out the balsamic flavor. The result is a sweet, tangy salad dressing. It's flavorful, so go light. One teaspoon will flavor a whole serving of salad."

This description uses humor to stress that the dressing is very potent. It tells you a little bit of background about where balsamic vinegar comes from and warns you of how little to use.

For Cream of Something Soup:

> "This recipe is for those times you have so many leftovers that even Mr. Tupper personally can't help you. Almost all leftovers from last night's dinner will work. I say "almost" because Cream of Lettuce and Lime Jello Soup is something you have to develop a taste for. But other than that, carrots, cabbage, potatoes, spinach, broccoli, zucchini and even left-over casseroles will work. (Cream of Green Bean With Crunchy Onion Casserole Soup is my favorite.)"

This humorous but very flexible recipe for leftovers needed a little explanation. It gives some ingredient suggestions and a warning of what not to use.

The introduction can be longer if needed and can even be longer than the recipe. Just keep it informative and entertaining. If it gets too long, turn it into a sidebar.

THE RECIPE

Recipe selection is the first step. Pick only your best recipes; never hold back good recipes for your "next cookbook." You want to be known for a book full of great recipes rather than a few good recipes and a lot of mediocre ones. Worry about your next cookbook after this one sells a million copies.

If a recipe sometimes fails, it has no business in your book. The "Sometimes Successful Soufflé" recipe is not what you want your legacy to be based on. If *you* can't get a recipe to work, how do you expect your readers to? If the recipe benefits from a little personal tweaking on the part of readers, that's fine; just don't expect them to appreciate a recipe that needs a factory recall.

There is an element of inertia you must overcome with any recipe: You must intrigue your readers with a recipe that will make them get up and actually prepare it. Even someone frantically looking for a recipe for dinner will look through numerous cookbooks before they choose something. Most cooks are looking for tasty, simple, easy, quick recipes. Be tough on each recipe. Can it be fixed in twenty minutes? Does it have eight or fewer ingredients? Can someone read the recipe once and remember how to fix it? If most of your recipes don't get yes answers to these questions, you need to go back over your recipes and cut the ones that meet the least of these criteria. Can you cut back on the number of ingredients by using mixes (spice mixes, box mixes, salad dressing, etc.)? Can you reduce cooking time by using quicker ingredients: canned beans over dry beans? Can you make the recipe simpler by combining steps, like adding dry pasta to a casserole instead of having to cook the pasta beforehand? Try it and see.

If your recipe would be ruined by canned ingredients, by all means stick with fresh. If your recipe requires time and attention for perfection, that's not a problem. Just remember that if you have too many recipes that require lengthy, labor-intensive preparation or rare ingredients not found in the average pantry or fridge, your book will be left on the shelf.

If a recipe has a few ingredients, takes ten minutes to fix, and turns out so flavorful and elegant that it seems like the cook has been working on it all week, it will be used over and over again.

Writing Recipes

Most aspiring cookbook authors will tell you their recipes are already written on cards in their recipe box. That's a little like saying you've written an adventure novel and then handing someone a AAA tour book. True, your recipes are written for your use, but not for others'. A few sentences and a lump of ingredients may not make much sense to someone who hasn't prepared the recipe a hundred times.

Clarity is very important. If you omit a word on a page in a novel, it probably won't change much. Skip a word in a recipe and it could have disastrous results. Be clear about whether to use baking powder or baking soda. "Quick fry" and "fry" are two very different techniques.

Keep your cooking terms simple. Say what you mean and explain if necessary. If you are saying "sauté," mean sauté. It's different from frying, pan frying, stir frying, or deep frying. To sauté means to dry cook with a small amount of fat in a pan or skillet over a high heat. Or to be safe, avoid the confusing term and say exactly what you mean. "Place a small skillet on a high heat. Add ½ teaspoon of butter. Add the onions. Stir them constantly until they turn golden." There is no doubt left in the reader's mind as to what to do.

The "until they turn golden" part tells how long to sauté. Telling the reader to cook something should always be followed by telling how long to cook it.

Keep your recipes simple. "Separate the whites and yolks of five eggs, beating the whites while setting aside the yolks and add to the mixture." That's not clear. Do you use the yolks or the whites? Use one command per sentence. "Separate five eggs. Set the yolks aside. Then beat the whites. Add the whites to the mixture." People who are not experienced cooks have enough trouble doing one thing at a time. Three or four commands per sentence can be very confusing.

It seems people who don't cook but just read cookbooks follow the directions in their mind very carefully. But the people who do cook don't preread recipes. Therefore you must put the instructions in a logical order. There are people who will prepare an entire recipe and only realize they are supposed to preheat the oven when they get to the end of the recipe and read "In an oven preheated to 325°. . . ."

If you put the instructions out of order, you make the process inconvenient for someone who is trying to follow the recipe. If exact timing is a factor, as with beaten egg whites (which will fall) or recipes using baking soda (which will react for a limited time), and instructions are out of order, the recipe may fail entirely. For example, a cake batter will deflate while the cook waits for the oven to preheat. Tell the reader to preheat the oven as the first step in the recipe, since that's what they logically should do first.

If you prepare part of a recipe and set it aside to work on another part, make it painfully obvious to readers. Tell them to set that part of the recipe aside or they may be making the cake and the icing in the same bowl.

Write your recipes in a user-friendly style. "Combine ingredients. Pour into shell. Bake 350°, 45 minutes" sounds like Arnold Schwarzenegger writing the *Terminator Cookbook*. "Combine all the ingredients. Pour them into the pie shell. Then bake the pie for forty-five minutes in the preheated oven" sounds less clinical. Removing words is a great time-saver when copying recipes for your files, but in a cookbook, minimal wording sounds impersonal. Cookbooks are a work of passion.

Consistency in wording is important. If you use "&" for "and," use it throughout the book. Alternating between the two will make your work seem cluttered. Use numbers in lists of ingredients and instructions. In reality, writing out numbers, like "three-quarters of a cup," is confusing. Using "¾ cup" makes the instructions clearer.

It's preferable to write out the units of measure. "Tablespoons," "teaspoons" and "cups" are much more clear than "T," "t" and "c." Many people born after 1950 were never taught to cook. To them the meaning of the abbreviations "T" and "t" seem like a secret learned only on initiation into the Secret and Crucial Order of the Odd Fork Whiskers.

Be specific with your measurements. How much is a "dash"? For each cook it's different. If your idea of a dash is ⅛ of a teaspoon and your reader's idea of a dash is a teaspoon, the recipe can turn out drastically different. A "pinch" is a little more specific, but with potent ingredients (such as cloves) even the variance between your pinch and the reader's pinch can throw the flavor off. Most households have a ¼ teaspoon measuring spoon; you can safely measure ⅛ of a teaspoon, which is half of the spoon. To me, ⅛ teaspoon is officially a pinch. If you need to go to a smaller measure, such as a "smidge," you may have to get creative with measure descriptions: "the last quarter inch of the wide flat end of a toothpick's worth" would probably be the next smallest.

A "squirt" varies in size. Measure out what you're squirting in drops if you have to. That may seem picky but if you're using concentrated ingredients, like essential oil of peppermint, four drops will ruin a batch of brownies with its overpowering flavor. If one of your measures ever seems so small or large that people will think it's a misprint, state it twice: "No that's not a typo, use only 3 (three) drops of this powerful flavoring."

Use real measures when you work and when you write. When I measured my silverware, I found the teaspoon was truly a teaspoon, but the soup spoon, which was assumed to be a tablespoon, was actually a teaspoon and a half. Never assume a drinking cup is equivalent to a measuring cup. Some teacups are half-cups and some mugs are a cup and a half.

I have an authentic Greek cookbook that I bought in Greece. Everything is measured in "teacups." Since some of the ingredients are specific to size, like "1 kilo of Feta," and everything measured with a teacup is of an unknown quantity, some recipes work and some don't.

It is assumed that measurements in a recipe are level and not heaping. If you work with heaping measures, you need to state that in the recipe. You might be better off to measure your heaping teaspoon out and find out how much it really is. Telling the reader that it's 2½ level teaspoons is more exact.

Different ingredients like flour and sugar "heap" differently. A heaping teaspoon of flour is about twice as much as a heaping teaspoon of sugar. Humidity causes things to heap differently too. A heaping teaspoon in

Florida is a different measure than a heaping teaspoon in Colorado. That's being picky, but with critical ingredients like spices, yeast and baking powder, you must be exact. It's attention to the little details that will make your recipes foolproof.

Be specific with your ingredients: Which cut of meat should be used? Stew beef cooks differently and tastes different than filet mignon. Should the meat be trimmed or not? Trimmed beef may not be as flavorful a cut as one with the fat left on. Do you mean canned, fresh or marinated artichokes? All three have very different flavors. How big a "can of pork and beans" do you mean? There's lunch size, regular size and family size. Using ounce measurements leaves no guesswork. What kind of pasta? Thick spaghetti and angel hair cook at very different rates.

Don't assume that because you buy skinless, boneless chicken breasts that everyone does. If your recipe says "chicken," some people may try the recipe with dark meat and gizzards. Say "1 large chicken breast (whole, skinless, boneless)" if that's what you mean.

Cookbook authors today must assume that each recipe is the first the reader has ever prepared. In many cases, you will be dealing with readers who don't cook regularly and who have never been taught how to cook. Don't mock people who don't know how to cook—that's a large portion of the cookbook-buying public. Don't say "prepare the rice as we *all* know how to do." We all don't. Tell them what you want them to do: "Place the rice in the boiling water. This keeps it from getting gummy. Reduce the heat to simmer and cover. Cook until almost all the liquid is absorbed. Remove the pan from the heat and let the rice set two minutes. Remove the cover and fluff by tossing the rice with a fork." You've explained technique and why you're doing what you're doing.

Don't insult readers' intelligence by talking down to them; just make your recipes easy for anyone to follow. You must discard your great cook attitude and wear a great teacher attitude. Read Julia Child or Paul Prudhomme. These great chefs don't talk down, but speak conversationally on the reader's level.

Keep the reader informed of how the recipe should look in mid-process or at the end of the preparation. If the cookie batter is stiff, you might want to tell them that it looks stiffer than normal cookie batter. People have a tendency to think cookie batter should have a certain consistency and may add more water if they think the batter is too thick; that, of course, would drastically change the outcome of the cookies. Let them know what something is supposed to look like, especially if it looks different than expected.

PROMOTING SAFETY IN THE KITCHEN

Kitchen health safety is becoming a bigger and bigger concern. Cookbook authors who advocate it will probably be smiled on by their publisher since there are fewer chances of lawsuits and since you are leading a trend. In the future, publishers may require that cookbook authors promote kitchen safety.

A lot of germs can be ingested by improperly prepared and improperly handled food. Here are some basic tips on safe food preparation that you can encourage in your cookbook. These can be incorporated quietly in recipes or can make good sidebars.

- Wash your hands before cooking. Bacteria and viruses can hide under your fingernails and be transmitted to food, so wash thoroughly.
- Meats are commonly contaminated. Thoroughly cook all meat to 165° to kill bacteria. When reheating, the temperature at the center of the food must reach 165° to kill any bacteria that's grown during storage.
- Avoid cross-contamination. This is where you contaminate one thing by bringing it into contact with another. An example: Meat is removed from a plate and grilled until the bacteria is killed. Then if it's put back on the same plate it's recontaminated. Use a fresh plate. Wash your cutting board after cutting meat: it can contaminate whatever else you cut on it. Even after cutting fruit and vegetables, you have to wash the board: the bacteria from the outside of a melon can contaminate the next thing you cut on the board.
- Thawing foods at room temperature encourages bacteria growth. Thaw them in the fridge or under cold (not hot) water.
- Use pasteurized milk products. Salmonella and E. coli love the protein of raw milk as a dividing ground.
- Cook your eggs. There are worse sources of salmonella than eggs, but why take chances?
- Use a sanitizing liquid. One of the most popular recipes on the cooking show I co-host is for a sanitizing solution given to us by Chef Paul Nichols, a head resort chef at Disney World. It's a teaspoon of bleach mixed with two cups of water. Clean every surface in your kitchen with it. It lasts for twenty-four hours in a spray bottle and

leaves no chlorine flavor on the food.
- Check with your local Board of Health. They usually have free pamphlets they'll send you.

RECIPE FORMATS

There are many different formats you can use to write a recipe. Here's a simple recipe from my *Fat-Free Real Food Cookbook*. The first version is the standard recipe. It starts with an ingredient list, which is followed by instructions.

Fat-Free Mocha Muffins

(Fix Time: 10 Minutes Finish Time: 40 Minutes. Makes one dozen.)

Warm muffins are good for breakfast or coffee. These are light, moist, and rich enough to be served to visiting royalty. But why invite the Queen over? When you've got food this good, why not eat it all yourself?

6 Egg Whites
¾ Cup Sugar
1 Tablespoon Vanilla
1 ½ Cups Flour
1 Teaspoon Salt
1 Teaspoon Baking Powder
¾ Cup Cocoa
3 Tablespoons Instant Coffee
1 Tablespoon Cinnamon
¼ Teaspoon Cloves (ground)
1½ Cups Marshmallow Creme

Preheat your oven to 325 Degrees. In a medium bowl mix all ingredients one at a time, stirring well after each addition.

Pour the batter into a muffin tin that has been lightly coated with cooking spray. Bake for 18-20 minutes.

This standard recipe format is compact and very clean looking. Its drawback is that complex recipes force readers to look at the list, look at the instructions, look at the list, look at the instructions. They can get lost, especially if it's the first time they've seen the recipe. There are other formats which make your recipes easier to follow. Readers usually opt for a recipe that is less confusing.

The next option is the conversational recipe. This is not used much anymore. The ingredients are listed in the middle of the "conversation." It's like someone telling you a recipe in the middle of a chat:

Fat-Free Mocha Muffins
(Fix Time: 10 Minutes Finish Time: 40 Minutes)
Warm muffins are good for breakfast or coffee. These are light, moist, and rich enough to be served to visiting royalty. But why invite the Queen over? When you've got food this good, why not eat it all yourself?

Preheat your oven to **325 Degrees**. In a medium bowl mix **6 Egg Whites**, and ¾ **Cup of Sugar**. Stir this well. Add **1 Tablespoon of Vanilla, 1½ Cups of Flour, 1 Teaspoon of Salt, 1 Teaspoon of Baking Powder, ¾ Cup of Cocoa, 3 Tablespoons of Instant Coffee, 1 Tablespoon of Cinnamon, ¼ Teaspoon of Cloves (ground)**, and **1½ Cups of Marshmallow Creme**. Stir well after each addition. Pour the batter into a muffin tin that has been lightly coated with cooking spray. Bake it for 18-20 minutes. There's breakfast.

This style of recipe is even more compact, but a little muddled looking. If you decide to use this style, it's best to put the ingredients in bold letters so none are missed. I've also used capitals to make the ingredients easier to spot.

My favorite recipe format is the following "as needed" style. The ingredients are listed as they are needed. The style was popularized by *The Joy of Cooking* in the 1930s and has held up well all these years. In the past you would have caught the eye of disdain if you didn't premeasure each ingredient and put it in its own little bowl before you started to make the recipe. Most cooks today don't want the extra dishes, so they measure and add each ingredient as they go. They find this recipe style very useful.

Fat-Free Mocha Muffins
(Fix Time: 10 Minutes Finish Time: 40 Minutes. Makes one dozen.)

Warm muffins are good for breakfast or coffee. These are light, moist, and rich enough to be served to visiting royalty. But why invite the Queen over? When you've got food this good, why not eat it all yourself?

Preheat your oven to **325 Degrees**.

In a medium bowl mix the following ingredients one at a time, stirring well after each addition:

6 Egg Whites
¾ Cup Sugar
1 Tablespoon Vanilla
1½ Cups Flour
1 Teaspoon Salt
1 Teaspoon Baking Powder
¾ Cup Cocoa
3 Tablespoons Instant Coffee
1 Tablespoon Cinnamon
¼ Teaspoon Cloves (ground)
1½ Cups Marshmallow Creme.

Pour batter into a muffin tin that has been lightly coated with cooking spray. Bake for **18-20 minutes**.

The advantage of this style of recipe is that there's no list to refer back to. It's the easiest format to follow. Bold, tabbed ingredients make the recipe easier to read.

To show you how this style looks when there are a lot of steps between ingredients, here's an excerpt from a mashed potato recipe:

Set a large pot half full of water to boil. In it place:
8 Medium Potatoes (peeled and cubed)
1 Teaspoon of Salt. When the potatoes will break when a fork is inserted into a cube, remove them from heat. Drain. Place in a large mixing bowl. Add:
¼ Cup of Buttermilk. Beat them with an electric mixer . . .

Also notice the preparation techniques in parentheses. Noting "(peeled and cubed)" after the ingredient tells the reader exactly what must be done in a minimum of words, and all on one line.

One other style of recipe which has almost vanished is the poem:

First you take a chicken leg
and dip it in some mixed-up eggs
then you dip it right in some
crunched and crumbled cracker crumbs
Once you've done both this and that
Cook it in some real hot fat
Take it when you go picnicking nothing beats cold fried
    chicken

I caution you that this is no longer considered a serious recipe format. If you're going to tackle a recipe poem, remember that clarity and light-heartedness are necessary to succeed. An entire book of recipe poems will get tedious unless it's heavily laced with illustrations, stories and other good writing to surround the poems. If you're sprinkling recipe poems into a regular cookbook, use them sparingly.

TESTING YOUR RECIPES
Once you've written a recipe, you must make sure it works every time. It's not enough that it works every time for you; it must work every time for everybody. Baked goods are especially vulnerable and might yield different results when someone else tries them. All recipes are susceptible to failure when they are out of your hands, so a few tests by others may tell you where the flaws exist in your recipe and in its execution.

Have your friends and acquaintances test your recipes in their kitchens. If five people test a recipe and one fails, find out if the friend made it properly. If four out of five fail, you will either need to rework the recipe or drop it from your book.

WHAT MAKES GOOD RECIPES GO BAD
When turning recipes into reality, mistakes are commonly made. Check your recipes for:
Lack of clarity
The wrong ingredient
The wrong technique
Incorrect oven temperature
Different cookware

Humidity effect
Altitude variation

Lack of Clarity

Watch while someone reads your recipe. You'll see if there's any confusion. Ask your friends who cook regularly to read your recipe and underline anything they find unclear. It also may help to have them explain the recipe to you in their own words. Sometimes you'll find points that seem crystal clear to both of you mean something completely different to each of you.

The goal is to have the reader prepare the recipe exactly the way you prepare it. If your wording is specific, the chances of that happening increase. Extra attention to clarity is required with complex recipes. A complex recipe is like a computerized car with all the gadgets and options; it just has more things that can go wrong.

The most heartbreaking thing for you as a cookbook author is when someone serves you a unique-looking dish you say, "What *is* this?"—only to find out it's one of your recipes.

The Wrong Ingredient

Imitation vanilla and vanilla extract are very different. Imitation vanilla contains water, real vanilla contains alcohol. That difference may completely change the result of your recipe. And then there's the drastic difference in taste.

Pillsbury flour and White Lily flour are made from two different kinds of wheat. White Lily may make a light, fluffy cake while Pillsbury may yield a more dense, moist cake.

Even the type of water you use plays a part. Try making bread with tap water and bottled spring water. Not only may the loaves look different but you can taste the difference.

Don't assume because you normally use cheap ingredients that the recipe will only work better if someone uses expensive ingredients. Cheap beer works best in chili. I tried to make my chili recipe with a beer that had passed a brewmaster's purity test instead of generic beer; it didn't turn out near as good with the expensive stuff.

If you find that only one certain brand of ingredient works, make sure you state that. If you make fudge with the finest sugar, it may work every time. Someone making your recipe with cheap sugar may never get the crystals to dissolve and wind up with fudge that goes to sugar every time. You might explain this to your readers to encourage them to use the correct ingredient.

The Wrong Technique

Simple variances in technique can ruin a recipe. For instance, egg flower soup only flowers if you add eggs to a hot liquid and stir in one direction. If you stir in both directions the egg "flowers" are shattered.

Dough that hasn't been "punched down" (pressed down to deflate it) may ruin a lovely braided loaf of bread. Don't assume the reader knows a standard technique for cooking.

Incorrect Oven Temperature

What if you're used to cooking in an oven that's 25° off? Some of your recipes may fail in a more accurate oven. Use an oven thermometer to find out if your oven is the correct temperature. Test your oven at 325°, 350°, and 375°, the most common cooking temperatures. If it's actually 375° when the dial on your oven says 350°, write 375° in your recipe, since that's what the correct temperature really is.

An oven that's been on for an hour will be warmer than one that's been on for twenty minutes, due to the absorbed heat in the walls. When testing recipes it's best to start with a cold oven and warm it as your directions say to make sure the recipe works. Most people will not have baked something in the oven before they try your recipe. Food placed on the lowest rack of the oven cooks the bottom of your dishes faster, while food on the highest rack bakes more evenly.

Convection ovens use moving hot air to cook. They cook faster than regular ovens. If your recipe works fine in a convection oven, try your recipe in a regular oven that's set twenty-five to fifty degrees hotter.

The number of variables in microwave ovens poses big problems. There are different wattages of microwaves, so some ovens cook very fast and others cook very slow. Those without a turntable heat food less evenly than those with one. A turntable can also slow down the cooking process. Some microwaves are also convection ovens, adding another variable. Also note that microwave convection and regular convection ovens cook very differently.

Microwave ovens usually range in power from 400 to 700 watts. Cooking time in low-watt models and high-watt models varies between

40 percent and 50 percent. A 700-watt microwave is 20 percent more powerful than a 600-watt and 40 percent more powerful than a 500-watt. Testing in a high-watt and a low-watt microwave oven might be necessary for your recipes.

Tip: Try cooking with your microwave at various power settings. The 50 percent power means the gun fires in short bursts and is on half the cooking time and off half the cooking time. The 50 percent power setting can cook foods more evenly. You can even cook and heat on the defrost setting. Also, if the oven doesn't have a turntable, turn your dish 90° halfway through the cooking process for more even heating.

Different Cookware

Glass, aluminum, steel and coated pans all cook differently. For instance, you may use an aluminum pan, but someone using a dark, nonstick steel pan can burn the same recipe while someone using an insulated pan can have it turn out underdone. Specify in your recipe which type of pan, skillet or other cookware to use.

Skillet selection has gotten very diverse. Some skillets have different metals for the interior, the exterior and the heating core. Some are coated with a nonstick surface and others are like a sponge to the food at high heats. All this means cooking results will be different in each skillet.

Heavy-bottomed skillets give off a uniform, constant heat. They also take a long time to warm up. A thin aluminum skillet can heat up in no time, burning part of the food while leaving the rest uncooked.

Some people get used to coated skillets and forget that anyone uses anything else. You might try your recipe in a few different skillet types. After all, your skillet may be very forgiving and your reader's skillet may not.

Humidity Effect

Living in a humid area, I know there is a big difference in chocolate chip cookies made in the summer or winter. Houses that are air-conditioned have a different humidity level than those that are not. Humidity can play a huge factor in baking success.

A little less liquid may be necessary during a humid summer. If humidity affects your recipe, note it. Have friends in other cities test your recipes to see if a different humidity level affects the result.

Altitude Variation

How high you are above sea level can sometimes change recipes. A little more liquid and a higher temperature or longer baking time may be necessary to get the same results as at sea level. The easy way to test your recipes in a different altitude is to post them with an Internet recipe newsgroup or in a chat room. At the bottom of the recipe, mention that you'd like to know the results from anyone at a higher or lower altitude. You will probably get several people who would be willing to try your recipes and let you know how they turn out. Most recipes are tested at an altitude within a few hundred feet of sea level.

THE RECIPE WRAP-UP

After the recipe is complete, you may want to provide some additional information. Is there a warning you need to give here? One of my recipes for a dry hot pepper shake mix was followed by a warning to use rubber gloves when handling hot peppers.

Here you can state variations on your recipe. In one of my fat-free cookbooks I included "Cheater's Upgrades" so that meat could be added to the recipes. Can you use soy milk instead of cream in the recipe if you're lactose intolerant? Can a canned ingredient be used instead of fresh for those in a hurry and, if so, how much time does it cut off the recipe?

Put some serving suggestions here. If it's a pesto sauce, make some suggestions for unique kinds of pasta for a good pasta salad. If it's a salad dressing, you can suggest how to use it for marinating meat. Something as simple as a recipe for perfect French fries can be enhanced by suggestions of bold sauces to dip them in.

Can the leftovers of the whole turkey be used as in Turkey Chimichangas the next night? If it's a simple recipe, tell how to prepare it in a paragraph instead of writing it out in a full-fledged recipe.

After each recipe in one of my books, I included Nutrition Facts labels. They look just like those on the back of food products. Today people want to know statistics about what they eat. It used to be they wanted to know how many calories a recipe contained. Now consumers want to know how many milligrams of salt and cholesterol, and how many grams of fat, carbohydrates and protein they're getting, too. Many computer recipe programs can calculate all this information when you type in your recipes.

4 YOUR COOKBOOK'S THEME

A book must be created around the recipes in it. You need a theme to make the book a cookbook and not a recipe box. If the book is to be given as a gift to family members, the theme is usually you or your family. There are stories you can tell about a recipe: how it came about, what happened when you fixed it, what the recipe reminds you of. As for content, only your best recipes should be included.

If you plan to sell your book, you're better off with a solid theme based on the food. Don't panic, there are an unbelievable number of themes:

- **Ingredient Themes:** a spice, canned soup, chocolate, wine, dairy products, drinks, etc.
- **Style of Cooking Themes:** grilling, canning, microwave, easy, quick, simple, etc.
- **Occasion or Seasonal Themes:** party, holiday, winter, etc.
- **Ethnic and Heritage Themes:** Asian, Greek, Shaker, etc.
- **Location Themes:** Rocky Mountains, Williamsburg, a restaurant, your neighborhood, etc.
- **Health Themes:** low sugar, high protein, heart smart, vegetarian, diabetic, etc.
- **The Cooking Bible:** A big book that contains every recipe imaginable or every recipe on a particular topic that you could ever want to cook.

Explore your theme. Make sure it's worthy of a whole book. Say you decide on a romance-themed cookbook. Food and love have always been inseparable. A romance cookbook can incorporate a romantic ambiance. Natural topics would be the romance countries of France, Italy and Spain. And some of the recipes can require no cooking for convenient execution. For example, an intimate table with a checkered tablecloth and a lone candle could be set with some cheese and a loaf of French bread. Recommend a good French wine, the name of a good CD or new age French music for the CD player, maybe even a little erotic e.e. cummings poem about Paris. You have a meal that will be remembered forever and you have a chapter for your book. Can you come up with ten of those? Can you give other tips on romance and food to fill out the book? Then you have a good theme for a cookbook.

FINDING A THEME

There are two ways to find a theme: (1) talk about what you know, and (2) talk about what people want to know.

What You Know

If you've never cooked Lithuanian flatbreads in your life, you probably aren't going to win a Pulitzer for *The Complete Authentic Lithuanian Flatbread Cookbook*. Evaluate your cooking skills. What are you good at? Some people are wizards at soups and can't make bread, even with a bread machine. Other people can't make a stew but can whip up great biscuits in no time. Some can grill best, some can make cookies best. Find your strength and base your theme on what you can do.

What style of cooking did you learn at home? Was yours a good old American kitchen or was it a passionate ethnic kitchen? Who cooked? Did you learn from both Mom and Dad? Did you learn from Grandma? Did you have a big change in your health that completely changed the way you eat? These factors probably have determined how you cook and have influenced your strengths in the kitchen, and they will help you decide on your recipe content.

You might know how to cook spaghetti correctly by watching Dad do it. Someone I know throws a hot piece of cooked spaghetti at the fridge door to determine doneness. If it sticks to the door, it's ready to eat. Including a little aside like that in your cookbook would not only be entertaining, but could be used to show off your technique in a spaghetti sauce recipe.

When trying to decide on a book's theme, evaluate what you cook. Many authors find they are not "well-rounded" cooks and have numerous thin sections of their recipe file and one thick one. That's not a hindrance but a strength to be exploited in your theme. If your recipe file is lopsided with desserts, you might try a dessert theme, even a dessert Bible.

Or get more specific: if more than half of your dessert recipes include chocolate as an ingredient, you might go for a chocolate theme.

If you have a dietary restriction and have a lot of recipes without the prohibited ingredient, there's your book. If you're lactose intolerant, come up with a cookbook that concentrates on lactose-intolerant recipes that substitute something else for dairy products. There are a limited number of people who need your specialized book, but those who do are starving for it. Niche markets may not create best-sellers, but they can create steady sellers that can be updated for years to come.

What People Want to Know

Successful professional cookbook authors follow trends and write cookbooks on a variety of topics. Most writers aren't professionally trained in all these areas, they are just good researchers of their topic. They find a trend. They research it in the library and online. They interview cooks who are pros on the topics. They modify existing recipes to make them more usable by home cooks. They work up their own new recipes. They consistently sell new cookbooks. You can too.

Home cooks and chefs are usually willing to share their technique. Most are happy to give out their recipes. Follow your curiosity: if you eat a good dish at someone's house, ask for the recipe. If you have a favorite dish at a restaurant, ask the chef how he or she prepares it. The chef might even be willing to let you come into the kitchen and watch how the dish is made. Most chefs and cooks are overjoyed that you're taking an interest and are flattered you asked. They also appreciate it when you give them credit.

You will learn a lot from the answers to your questions and from watching good cooks and successful chefs work. They know what makes good food. If their skill impressed you, it will probably impress other people when you write about it. Cookbook authors are most successful when they're still willing to learn.

Groups putting together charity cookbooks usually take submitted recipes, organize them and print a cookbook. This extremely general, haphazard type of cookbook will sell a small number of copies. However, a *themed* charity cookbook is more marketable to the public and not just to group members. Pick a theme for your cookbook and have people in the charity submit recipes on that theme. This way you can produce a new fundraising cookbook based on a different theme every year or two.

Another common charity theme is to do a cookbook featuring the recipes of a local restaurant or restaurants. Many restaurants are happy to donate the recipes, as it's free publicity for them. They also are usually willing to help promote your book and possibly sell it in the restaurant.

If the theme of your cookbook and the charity it's benefiting are distinctly different, put information on the charity in sidebars in your book. A Mexican resort cookbook benefiting multiple sclerosis may seem very confusing otherwise.

PUTTING IT ALL TOGETHER

Let's put together a cookbook. Here is a theme example that fits all types of cookbooks.

Say you're from the Pacific Northwest. Great-Grandpa was a logger. You have Great-Grandma's recipes that have inspired your family traditions of cooking. You look at the market and see all the health-oriented cookbooks that remove fat, sugar, cholesterol and all those other ingredients that make food taste good. As with any knee-jerk reaction to medical research there is an equally opposite knee-jerk rejection of the data. The market is ripe for a book that emphasizes the joy of fat-laden foods. As loggers ate up to eight thousand calories a day, Great-Grandma definitely knew about heavy food.

So this book is one that you would give to family as a gift. It's a biography of Great-Grandma and Great-Grandpa. It is also historical. Could it also be used as a charity cookbook? Sure. If you were a supporter of the Loggers Union, a museum for logging, or even a group that is trying to save an old mill as a historic landmark, your book could come to the rescue. How about it being a best-seller? If your theme is done well, it's probably strong enough to sell on the public market.

Great-Grandma's Logger Cookbook has no snap to it. There is nothing in the title that would make someone pick it off a shelf at a bookstore and open it up. Give it a title that has some novelty to it. *The Lumberjack Diet* not only appeals to people who are interested in history, but as a novelty it will appeal to dieters and nondieters alike. A picture of Great-Grandpa on the cover smiling with his ax or saw would work well.

You can use Great-Grandma's recipes by themselves or add your own. Some recipes may need modification due to ingredient changes. If a recipe calls for beaver or bear lard, you'll want to let readers know if they should use pork lard or if shortening, butter or oil will work just as well.

For historical purposes, you may want to use the exact wording Great-Grandma did in her recipes. You can follow this with any notes needed to clarify. If the book is for the masses, you may want to reword the recipes in a simple, logical and modern way for clarity. Explain any cooking terms or the meaning of other words that have become cloudy over the years. If Great-Grandma was of Chinook ancestry and talked about lots of "muckamuck" at a gathering, she either means "food" or "logging brass." Remember that historical preservation may actually benefit from your clear writing, as opposed to leaving Great-Grandma's recipes as puzzles from the past for future generations to try to solve.

If you want to be a historical purist and just use the original recipes, that's fine. Or you may want to add your own recipes that fit the same mold or maybe even healthy, updated versions of Great-Grandma's recipes.

The theme of this book opens up a lot of possibilities for recipe introductions and sidebars. You may want to talk about your ancestors in the introduction to each recipe and give some sidebars about logging in general. Or you may want to do the opposite and put the family history in sidebars and the general logging information in the introduction to the recipes.

Whether for family or for the general public, your book's thoroughness would benefit from doing some research into logging. The better you set the scene of the times, the more the reader can appreciate the recipes. Start with what you can find out from family and friends. Old scrapbooks, bibles, even the margins of Great-Grandma's cookbook are good sources. Go to the library and research logging, or look it up on the Internet. You might also visit a logging exhibit. Interesting statistics and details will keep people reading. The more well-researched the book is, the more appeal it will have.

If you have some amazing family stories and have found other lumberjack stories, they will add flavor to the scene you're setting of the late 1800s in the Northwest woods. Describe the living conditions. What were the clothes like? Where did your grandparents live? How did Great-Grandpa meet Great-Grandma? Make it fascinating. If there was a cake that united the two, tell about it in the introduction to the recipe.

Was the same meat available year round or were some recipes seasonal? A berry pie made with fresh berries obviously would be seasonal. What did lumberjacks do in the summer? Did they go on vacation? What were the summertime festivities? How did they brave the winters in the Cascades?

The sidebars can present an enthralling history of your family and the profession that Great-Grandpa gave his life to. Talk about wages, the company he worked for, how Great-Grandma and the ladies at the time dressed, what they gossiped about, the U.S. and Canadian logging industry in general and how much wood was cut.

Keep your sidebars as self-inclusive as possible. One on how to dress a bear or a beaver would be fascinating. (You *do* need to keep it in the meat section and not put this sidebar in with desserts.) How did they stretch ingredients when supplies were low? Some of the recipes may even be tailored around low supplies. Look for ones that mention use of an ingredient "when available" or recipes that are loose with amounts. Every woman who cooked at the time was proud of her ability to make-do and prepare good food with the ingredients she had.

And don't lose sight of your theme. This *is* a diet book. But a little research will show that most lumberjacks were not fat despite their massive calorie and fat intake. Talk about the exercise that kept them from obesity. Working from sunup to sundown played a part. Talk about how heavy the axes were. Give a tutorial on the proper way to swing an ax. Tell about the festivities at lumberjack competitions. Just how does one keep from falling in the water while "logrolling"? Tell how to logroll. Tell about how the term "logrolling" became a political term for cooperation. Tell how "logrolling" is not really called logrolling at all, but "birling."

Get detailed. Talk about how the sport of birling originated about 1840 from the gutsy lumberjacks who pried the logjams loose as they sped down a raging river. Talk about the rules and how the goal was to make your opponent lose his balance and fall into the water. (Two out of three falls is officially a match.) Tell about how the competition evolved into "stunt rolling." Educate and entertain.

The subject matter of your theme and how it's handled will make the difference between a book that's of interest to you only and a book that's of interest to many people.

The Lumberjack Diet is a hypothetical cookbook. Let's examine a real book.

As I researched my cookbooks and experimented with recipes, I watched the eager eyes of my two-year-old son, Tristan, as I worked.

Soon he was cracking eggs without getting shells in the batter. He was kneading dough. He was wearing oven mitts and stir-frying dinner.

It occurred to me that the wonderful bonding experience of a parent and child cooking together was disappearing because parents no longer knew how to cook. But my son and I were doing it, so why couldn't we teach others? The result was the coauthoring of *The "Hey Mom I Like This" Cookbook—Lower Fat, Lower Sugar Recipes for Kids and Parents to Fix Together*. The project was a blast. Tristan contributed some of his own original recipes.

The book was designed for parents and kids to use together. Each recipe included drawings of how to prepare the food. That way a two-year-old who couldn't read could still make the recipes. Children who could read also benefited from seeing how the recipe was made. I was surprised to find that parents of college kids were buying the book as their offspring's first cookbook.

The book's recipes were formulated to be lower-fat and lower-sugar, but not low-fat and low-sugar. I had determined that if you took all the fat and sugar out of the food, kids—the most severe critics—wouldn't touch it. So we left enough of the good stuff in to keep the flavor in.

There's the theme, now how to pull it off.

The introduction explained the concept of the teaching cookbook to the parents. It presented "Tips For Improved Eating" that showed how to get your kids to be better eaters. I included tips like: "Make sure you're willing to eat what you want your child to eat. Children learn by example."

I used a basic sans serif typeface (see Glossary) for comments that were intended for the adults and a legible kidscrawl font for text intended for the children to read.

The first chapter was on kitchen safety. It showed little "OUCH!" signs pointing to drawings of dangerous things in the kitchen, like a stove burner, a knife, a food processor, a grater and a toaster. Each had an explanation of why you should be careful with it.

The second chapter was "No Cook Recipes." The order of the chapters was from simple to hard recipes, and those without heat seemed the easiest and safest for the younger children. We included recipes for making banana puppets, using cookie cutters to make cheese art with cheese slices and making burritos, as well as instructions on how to make yogurt cheese and grow sprouts. "Pretzel Grape Appetizers" opened chapter two. These were made simply by jamming a pretzel stick into a grape and using it as a handle. The footnotes, in small letters across the bottom of the page, gave parental tips:

> "A Tristan Original. It's advised that these appetizers don't sit long. The grapes will make the pretzels soggy. But they do well in the freezer as Grapesicles."

Chapter three got into simple recipes that used heat and knives but were easy enough for a young child to do with close supervision. "Microwave S'Mores," "Tristan's Mashed Ranch Potatoes," and "Easy Cheese Pizza" were followed by a story called the "Land Where They Banned Spinach."

Remember the story of "stone soup?" Three mistrusted soldiers come to town and can't get anyone to give them food. They cleverly say, "That's okay, we'll just make some stone soup." The curious folk provide a huge pot with some water and the soldiers put a stone in it. The soldiers say, "This soup sure would taste good if we had some carrots." So someone gets a carrot. They do the same with other vegetables until they have a pot of vegetable soup big enough to feed the town, and of course they share it and of course everybody loves them. The End.

You can't get kids to eat vegetable soup, but if you tell them that story, sterilize a rock from the garden, and make a pot of stone soup, they're dying to try it. I took the same premise and wrote an illustrated story about a boy in the Kingdom of Mundania who ousts the king because the boy and everyone else hates the "you must eat spinach" decree. The boy becomes king and is loved—until everyone becomes anemic. So to save the day, he finally goes to the town square and tries spinach. He says "It's not great, but it's not that bad." The food in the story is "Mundanian Salad," "Fried Bananas," and "Spinach Speckled Bread." I had reports that the accompanying recipes actually got kids to try spinach. The footnote to "Gilroy's Fried Bananas and Spinach" reads:

> "If kids won't eat this, you may as well give up on cooked spinach. One tablespoon of honey can be substituted for the brown sugar. Fresh lime juice is recommended. Always use fresh spinach: canned or frozen spinach tastes like hay. Children don't like the taste of hay."

The next chapter contained advanced recipes: "Raisinman Cookies," "Rainbow Pudding," and "Monkey Bread." There was also a poem about "Gretta's Green Pasta" and the recipe to make spinach pasta. Kids loved the activity of making pasta and tried something with spinach in it.

From the footnote for the "Monkey Bread" recipe:

> "This is a good recipe to make when your child has a friend over on a rainy day. If you're going to make this bread as a morning activity, it's probably best to make the dough the night before. That way you're already to the fun part when the company arrives or the kids wake up."

I think that gives you the idea of how the book was created from the theme out and each recipe was designed and chosen to support the theme. What themes could you use for your cookbook?

5 ORGANIZING YOUR RECIPES

There needs to be some sensible order to your recipes. It all comes down to usability. What's the criteria for how your chapters will be ordered? The standard is the order used in eating:

Appetizers
Entrées
Desserts

Or you might try:
Breakfast
Lunch
Dinner

If your cookbook contains fifty recipes, this will work. That's about sixteen recipes per chapter. Another option for chapter order is seasons:

Spring
Summer
Fall
Winter

If your book will have more than fifty recipes, you will probably want more specific chapter headings:

Appetizers
Entrées
Side Dishes
Desserts
Snacks

You can also do a chapter for each month of the year. A fresh vegetable cookbook can follow the planting season and give recipes for the time of year that certain foods are ripe:

Sprouts
Early Harvest
Main Harvest
Late Harvest
Winter Canning

If writing a romance cookbook for dating, you could break up the chapters into stages of dating:

First Contact (recipes with no onions or garlic)
Winning Over (fun recipes to prepare together)
Intimate Contact (aphrodisiacs)
Special Occasions (meeting parents, engagement, anniversary)

If you divide your cookbook into chapters on food type and have five or more recipes in a specific area, you might want to give them their own heading. Headings include, but are not limited to:

Beans & Pulses	Pancakes
Beef	Pasta
Beverages	Pastry
Breads	Pies
Cakes & Frostings	Pizzas
Candy	Puddings
Cookies	Salad Dressings
Eggs	Salads
Fish	Sandwiches
Fowl	Sauces
Fruit	Soups
Game	Vegetables
Grains	Waffles

If the cookbook is very specific, such as a meat, poultry and fish cookbook, you might divide it into sections that go from dark to light or light to dark meat: Fish, Seafood, Chicken, Turkey, Pork, Ostrich, Beef, etc.

Other options are organization by:

Menu: If you're presenting four or five recipes that make a complete meal, each meal can be its own chapter.

Ethnic Group: In a multi-ethnic cookbook: Greek, Italian, Oriental, etc. An Oriental cookbook may be divided into Thai, Chinese, Vietnamese, etc.

Products: An all-dairy cookbook, for example, could be divided into milk, yogurt, sour cream, cream, etc.

Cooking Techniques: No-bake, bake, grilling, microwaving, etc.

Ease of Preparation: Generally you move from easy to difficult recipes. Would your book benefit from chapter divisions organized by length of cooking time (fifteen minutes or less, fifteen to thirty minutes, thirty minutes to an hour, over an hour)? How about dividing by number of ingredients? (Fewer than five, five to ten, ten and over.) Or how about simple, intermediate, difficult recipes? Ease-of-preparation divisions will sit well with impatient cooks and the book editors who want to please them.

THE OTHER INGREDIENTS

The notes, anecdotes, background information, etc. that accompany the recipes in your book give it personality. Look at successful cookbooks and you'll notice a lot of personable, well-researched writing surrounds those recipe ingredient lists and instructions. Take that away and you'll see how bland the great book looks.

Information With the Title

What information about the recipe do people want quick access to? Put it right below the title. In my books I have been diligent with "Fix Times" and "Finish Times." Fix time is the actual labor-intensive preparation time. Some recipes may take an hour to make, but the labor-intensive part of the recipe may take only five minutes. For things like quick breads, the fix-time and finish-time numbers let readers know that if someone calls and says they're dropping by in an hour, they can spend five minutes mixing up the spice bread and the other fifty-five minutes of the hour cleaning before the warm, fragrant bread is done and the guests arrive. The finish time is the hour this recipe takes from the start until the oven door opens. If the guests will be there in thirty minutes, you know to pick a quicker recipe. This time information is very useful and makes recipe selection practical for readers.

Another piece of decision-making information that can be inserted just below the title is the number of servings. A reader looking to feed a specific number of people will find this very useful. State the amount the recipe makes, measured in cups, pieces or servings.

Some cookbook authors develop their own system of symbols to give readers quick access to useful information. Carol Gelles in *1,000 Vegetarian Recipes* boxes in the letters "L," "O," "LO," and "V" to show dietary restrictions. "L" means the recipe is lacto- (contains dairy products). "O" means the recipe is ovo- (contains eggs). "LO" means the recipe is ovolactarian (contains dairy and eggs). "V" means the recipe is Vegan (contains neither). This may not be useful to most people, but to the vegetarians the book is themed for, the markings are very valuable.

Other symbols you might use are an exclamation point for quick recipes, a heart for heart-smart foods, a smile for healthy fare, a sun for light dishes, or a piece of bread with a number in it for the number of diabetic carbohydrate exchanges the recipe contains. If you're using symbols, make sure you include a legend to tell readers what they mean. It wouldn't hurt to have a legend on every other page.

In *The Barbecue Bible* Steven Raichlen lists at the beginning of each recipe a translation of the title, the country the recipe is from, the method of grilling, amount of time required for advance preparation, and any special equipment needed that might not be in most pantries. Information like this could all go later in the recipe, but by putting it at the beginning, you make your book more useful.

Chapter Introductions

Each chapter benefits from an introduction. It can be a paragraph to a few pages. *The Portable Feast*, a picnic cookbook by Diane D. MacMillan, uses some quotes about picnics from literature to adorn the chapter pages. This is also a good place for illustrations.

If it's a chapter on pies, you could tell readers about the characteristics of a good pie you learned from judging a pie-baking contest. Talk about why pies fail. Give a little history of the pie and explain that it was one of the first fast foods dating back to the thirteenth century. Is there a good family pie story? A chapter introduction should say something more than "here's a bunch of pie recipes." Give the chapter some purpose. Entice the reader who has never baked a pie to try.

The following briefly introduced the sauce section of one of my cookbooks:

A Sauce Tour of the Orient

The number of Oriental sauces is noggin jittering. Soy sauce is the basis for most. (Soy sauce is the Orient's source of salt.) A light soy sauce is recommended because a regular soy is very strong. Superior brand soy from China is probably the best, and the cheapest. If using a regular soy, dilute it half sauce and half water.

This short introduction takes some of the mystery out of Oriental sauces by letting readers know that most of them have a soy base. It also lets them know why the sauces are so popular: since they provide salt in the diet. It recommends which sauce to use and gives a practical tip on how to dilute an overpowering sauce.

These general tips pertain to all the sauces in the section. The introduction is a good place to give an overview of what's to follow.

Sidebars

Sidebars are now so common that cookbooks would look bare without them. These little asides can contain entertainment or all kinds of information for the cook: tips, suggestions, even related short recipes. They are the subplot of your cookbook: they present parallel information. Those who are skilled with sidebars can use them to effectively incorporate food-related and nonfood-related material into their cookbooks.

Sidebars can also pertain specifically to a recipe. You can make a recipe more clear by moving nonessential material to a sidebar, or if part of the process is difficult and confusing, you can use a sidebar to explain it. Let's take the example of a banana ice cream recipe. Here are some sidebars you might write that deal specifically with a recipe:

Serving Suggestion: Tell readers they can make great banana split ice cream sandwiches by putting it between chocolate graham crackers. Suggest sauces: something expected like chocolate and something different like caramel.

Use of the Dish in Other Foods: Ice cream makes great French toast. Talk about the flavor a banana ice cream would bring to this breakfast food. Give some suggestions for a syrup that would compliment "Banana Ice Cream French Toast."

Choosing Ingredients: Tell the reader how to determine when bananas are at their sweetest: when spots first start to appear on the skin. Tell them the differences in cream. Should they use a heavy whipping cream? Will half-and-half yield an acceptable result? What happens if they substitute honey or brown sugar for the white sugar?

Tips From the Pros: Talk to people who make ice cream both professionally and at home. Use their tips for making the perfect quart of ice cream.

Avoiding Failure: Cite the most common reasons why ice cream fails. You might even have a failure you can relate.

Taking Care of Your Ice Cream: Explain the best method of storing homemade ice cream so it doesn't turn into a block of ice.

Explain the Process: Tell how ice cream is actually sweetened and flavored cream with tiny ice crystals in it, and that the main difference between soft-serve and regular ice cream is that the soft-serve process never lets the crystals get big. Tell why cheap ice cream is cheap and weighs less: it's full of air.

Healthy Alternatives to the Recipe: Talk about low-fat modifications, sugar-free ice cream, ways to add more protein, a dairy-free version for the lactose intolerant that uses soy or rice milk.

Choosing Equipment: Tell what to look for in an ice cream freezer. Recommend a few brands of freezers you've had success with. Tell them the truth: that the upscale, small-capacity, cool-looking, hand-crank models are just torture devices. Give techniques for making ice cream without an ice cream freezer.

Favorite Flavors: Do a little research and find out some celebrities' favorite flavors of ice cream.

Ice Cream Stats: What's the most popular flavor of ice cream? (It's still vanilla.) How much do we consume? (1.5 billion gallons a year in the U.S.)

History: Did the ice cream cone actually come about when they ran out of dishes at the 1904 World's Fair? (Most likely.)

Shatter a Myth: Pasta was already in Italy when Marco Polo returned from China, but he did bring back the recipe for ice cream. (It's true.)

Ice Cream Tales: Funny ice cream stories from personal experience are good, especially if the cookbook is intended for family members. You can heighten the humor by doing the story as a news report:

Dateline Stow, Ohio. Weekend plans at the Smith summer place went awry. . . ." Or you can do it as a police blotter report: "4:15 P.M.: A small explosion was reported by neighbors in the vicinity of 306 Lakeside. 4:23 P.M.: Officer arrived on the scene to discover family members still covered with ice cream. 4:27 P.M.: The perpetrator of the incident, one known as 'Uncle John,' admitted to the officer that when the ice cream freezer motor was discovered inoperational he had rigged a diesel generator to the ice cream freezer. . . ."

There are many options. Sidebars can also tell a story not directly related to the recipe. On the page with a taco salad recipe I included a sidebar called "Flatulence Facts" and told how to reduce the gas-producing ability of beans.

Sidebars are short stories, mini technical books, tiny trivia guides, whatever you want them to be. They really add their own flavor to the cookbook.

Many of the elements that used to appear in the appendix of a book now become sidebars. For instance, you could break up cooking terms into numerous "Cooking Terms 101" sidebars and sprinkle them throughout the book.

Your sidebars should inform, entertain or both. Here is a list of just a few general sidebar possibilities:

How to Fold Napkins
Microwave Hints
A Cooking Measure Conversion Chart
A Calorie Counter
Sources for Ingredients
Fresh Herbs vs. Dried Herbs
Defatting Broth
How to Cook Rice
Cooking With Alcohol
Wine Suggestions
Party Suggestions
How to Soften Frozen Butter
Leftover Suggestions
Dieting Tips
Tips on Feeling Better When You Stand on the Bathroom Scale

Seasoning Cast Iron
Picking the Right Knife for the Job
When to Use a Thermometer
Cutting Brownies and Not Destroying Coated Pans
How to Choose Vegetables at the Market
How to Thicken Sauces and Gravies

Of course, sidebars can just as easily be turned into an appendix.

Make sure to list your sidebars in the index so they are easy to find. Sidebars can be short, one-line notes or they can be a page-long story. The space you have available on a page will probably determine length. The information should be condensed:

Defatting Broth

Short of a special defatting pitcher, the easiest way to defat meat broth is to chill it. Saturated fat hardens and floats when cold. It can then easily be scooped off. If using canned broth, keep it in the fridge. Most of the fat will be stuck to the lid when you open it.

That's one paragraph of fifty-four words. Informational sidebars need to be to the point.

Cooking Rice

The proper way to cook rice is to toss it into boiling water with a little bit of salt. Putting rice into cold water and then heating it up will cause the cooked rice to be gummy.

That's thirty-seven words that you could include in the recipe, but offsetting it in a sidebar helps the recipe flow better. You can be a little more flexible with entertaining sidebars.

In my first book, I wrote a humorous sidebar to fill a page at the end of a chapter. In fat-free cooking, you have a lot of leftover egg yolks. The sidebar gave a legitimate suggestion on what to do with these yolks followed by a list of humorous uses. I received such great response to the sidebar that I included this update in my second book.

Revenge of "What To Do With Your Egg Yolks"

- Feed them to stray dogs that roam your neighborhood. As part of a beautification campaign, even rabid, roaming packs of canines will have beautiful, shiny coats.
- Mix 12 egg yolks with 2 sticks of butter, 3 cups of sugar, 1 teaspoon of vanilla, 3 cups of flour, and 1 cup of cream. Bake at 325 degrees for an hour. It makes the most delicious pound cake that contains 231 grams of fat per slice. Give it as a gift to your worst enemy just before he goes in for his cholesterol check.
- Dry an egg yolk and shellac it to make a stunning brooch. It accents both blue and green outfits. Mr. Blackwell will give you a thumbs up. Martha Stewart will be jealous that she didn't think of it first.
- Put a dozen yolks in a Mason jar. Then call that tabloid TV show "A Really Inside Hard Current Edition." When the reporter comes, tell her it's a jar of sun juice given to you by aliens who siphoned it out of a star personally, and gave it to you as a housewarming gift. They will pay you mongo bucks for your exclusive story.
- Found your own cable-TV, mail-order, yolk-worshipping religion. Send everyone who mails you a love offering their own yolk that's been personally annointed-by-the-appointed. It's a relic their family will cherish for generations.
- Hand one out your car window to panhandlers who dress as homeless people and carry "will work for food signs." Then say, "Here's your food, come paint my house!"

Sidebars can be written in a cookbook that's strictly for family. This one tells a true story. (And I know it's true because I was there when it happened. So don't be starting an urban myth with my family's history!)

The $2500 Pie

The family reunion had been a disappointment for Uncle Bobby. He got there a little late since he had to come the farthest of any of us. By the time he arrived, Aunt Helen's incredible chocolate cream pie was gone. And yes, I was one of the guilty parties. Her vanilla creme was very good and there were two of those left, but Bobby had a hankering so bad for that rich chocolate pie of hers he asked Aunt Helen to make another.

She laughed and said that she wouldn't do that even for an airline ticket to visit him in Florida. So he offered her a ticket and one to Mom and one to Aunt Thelma, since he knew she didn't want to be the one who took their free trip away from them. She baked the pie. He sat down and ate it. All three of them went south for the winter.

There's a family tale brought to life. It's a complete story despite being only two paragraphs long. Of course, the pie recipe that would follow this tale no longer seems like just an ordinary chocolate pie. Family stories about a recipe can make the food seem special.

Sidebars can also be written in installments. There is no reason why you can't have a story or an interview recurring in sidebars, noting the page where it continues. It can even be a novella, filling space at the end of recipes. You can use these sidebars to sustain your theme throughout the book.

6 A PRIMER ON COOKBOOK LAYOUT

If your cookbook is sold to a publisher, they will probably handle the layout for you. As a self-publisher, keep in mind that layout can make a bigger difference in the look of the finished book than the print quality. Open a successful cookbook from your bookshelf. Most likely the layout is simple, clean and classy.

The content order is pretty much standard for all cookbooks:
Title Page (optional)
Copyright Notice and International Standard Book Number (ISBN)
Dedication
Thank You's and Acknowledgments
Table of Contents
Foreword
Introduction
The Recipes
Appendix
Index

The title page includes the title of the book, the name of the author and the name and location of the publisher.

For legal purposes, the copyright notice should go at the front of the book. The ISBN should be printed in the front of the book and on the back cover to make it easy to find, since this is the number bookstore employees use to order books. To save on printing costs, the dedication, acknowledgments, copyright and ISBN number can all go on the same page.

The dedication page contains the name of the person to whom the book is dedicated. Self-publishers sometimes skip this. From personal experience, I will urge you not to. I dedicated my first book to my father, and he died unexpectedly two weeks after I handed him the first copy I printed. Use the dedication for a loved one or someone who made you the cook you are today. One sneaky trick that self-publishers can do is to print up a dedication page for each person they send a review copy to.

The acknowledgments page is the place to thank anyone who gave you recipes or helped you put your book together. Of course you can also thank the family to keep them from getting a complex.

The table of contents lists the title of each chapter and the chapter's beginning page number.

The foreword is usually by someone other than the author. If the book will never be seen outside your family, you might want your spouse or a relative to write the foreword. It can be about the book, the family, you or the two of you. If the book is to be sold to the general public, it's a good idea to enlist the talents of someone prominent for the foreword. Local cooking columnists and newspaper food editors are good people to ask. They command a lot of respect in your local area.

If you want someone more well-known nationally, use your connections. Is there someone local who is known nationally? Since my first cookbook was about fat-free cooking, I contacted Lilias Folan, the yoga instructor on PBS, who lived nearby and boldly asked for her help. Though she didn't know me, she was glad to help.

After I wrote my first book, my family and I were vacationing in Maine and found an unbelievable bed and breakfast in the rural countryside. The owner of the Sunset House asked me about my first book and told me that her husband was into cooking. Carl Johnson was wearing an Izod shirt and jeans when I met him. He seemed incredibly knowledgeable about fat-free sauces for someone just "into" cooking. It turned out he was the executive chef at the prestigious Bar Harbor Inn. Right then and there, I enlisted him to do the foreword to my next book.

It doesn't hurt to ask someone you don't know to do a foreword. The worst they can do is turn you down. Well okay, they could do worse, like put Jell-O in your gas tank, but they probably won't. If you are afraid to ask in person or on the phone, write a letter or E-mail your humble request.

The introduction of your book can be written by yourself or someone else. If the book's theme needs an introduction, this is the place to do it. An introduction written by a noted expert works well. For instance, if your book is a dairy-free cookbook, an introduction by a dietitian who can point out the health benefits of your book would be a good choice. The more well-known the expert is and the more credentials the person has, the better.

The appendices are a good place to put necessary but cumbersome information. This is the place for explanation of cooking techniques, large charts like How to Blanch Vegetables, Calorie Tables, Menus, Pressure Cooking Times, Metric-Imperial Measurement Conversions, Roasting Temperatures, etc.

The index is vital to the book. Even if your book includes only fifty recipes, an index will be the most-used section of the book.

PAGE LAYOUT

Desktop publishing programs make a lot of people think they are professional layout artists. They give you a lot of powerful tools that can be dangerous in the wrong hands. It's like users have been turned loose in a construction yard and they're using a pile driver to drill screw holes. Overbearing, clashing colors; extravagant, unreadable type; and lopsided, confusing layouts have become the norm among self-publishers who can afford the cost of using the computer programs. Even some big print houses have become guilty of hasty, tacky layouts.

If you're going to do it yourself, anything you learn about art will improve your layout skills. Your first step may be taking a class in art appreciation. The basic concepts you learn by examining what great artists have done correctly can give you a more well-rounded art background. Check out "art appreciation" on a Web search engine and see what pops up. Learning about balance, color selection, color coordination, etc., is valuable knowledge that can be used to make your book layout look very professional.

Look at other cookbooks that are on the best-seller lists. Examine their layout techniques to keep up on the trends so your book looks up-to-date and is competitive.

The first lesson in graphic design is: never show your ignorance. Those of us who are untrained in graphic arts may not be able to recognize the subtleties of color, the nuances of a typeface, or the finer points of balancing a recipe and an image on the page. However, most everyone can tell when colors clash, when a typeface is illegible, or when a page looks unbalanced. Use common sense if you don't have graphic training and decide to do your own layout.

Recipe Position on a Page

Generally, recipes are positioned at the top of the page with the sidebar (if any) at the bottom. However, recipes can be positioned on the left side of the page with the sidebar at the right or at the end of a page or the end of the second page after a long setup. Just don't try to put too many items on a page. A recipe, a sidebar and an illustration are about all you can put on a page before it starts looking cluttered. If you use these three elements on the same page, the illustration or photo usually looks better at the top.

Color

Color is enticing. It can give your recipes a good "feel." It's the overuse of color that's a problem. Take the example of a recipe with neon teal letters on a hot pink background. Not only is it hard to read with the letters leaping back and forth out of the background, but the color combination makes some people physically ill. A cookbook that makes you nauseous will not be remembered as a good cookbook.

Psychologists have spent years researching which colors are the most appetizing. Red is the most appealing. It's worked on Coke cans quite well. Lately, however, we have grown more accepting of other colors. For instance, blue was never used with food until the past few years. Now it has become very acceptable as a color for kids' drinks and sports drinks. Even in solid form, like M&M's, blue food is now being accepted. Still, food usually looks better on a red plate than it does on a blue plate.

Basically, here is how colors affect us:

Red, yellow and orange are warm, active colors. Warm hues are very appealing to the eye. Warm is also inviting. Women generally prefer red.

Green is a neutral to cool color that symbolizes freshness. Recently it has been used on boxes to symbolize health and low-fat content.

Blue is a cool color. It symbolizes cold and refreshment. Men tend to like blue.

White symbolizes cleanliness. White and cream tend to be the best colors for paper stock.

Today's trend in cookbooks is toward bold colors. Sometimes the backgrounds clash with themselves and with the color of the fonts and photos. The more innovative you try to be, however, the more you need the help of a graphic designer.

Tip: Graphic design students tend to try to be very bold in their work.

A seasoned designer will charge more, but may be worth the extra money to create a tastefully laid out book. If you do get a graphic design student to help, it's best to closely monitor progress. Explain that the book will be an exercise in subtlety, not a chance to show off the latest design method.

The appetizing aspect of paper stock and ink choices are often overlooked. Natural food cookbooks from the 1970s have a great visual appeal. Why? The small print houses drifted from convention. They used cream and light brown, rough-textured paper stock with dark brown inks, which gave the books a very wholesome look. The earthy fonts, handwritten recipes and line drawings added to the look. It's still being copied by big publishers today.

Fonts

The number of fonts available for typesetting is vast. But that doesn't mean you should use too many different fonts on the same page. Books that look clean and are easy to read usually a maximum of three or four fonts per page. Sometimes they use only three or four fonts throughout the whole book. There is nothing wrong with using a snazzy font for the title, a sans serif font for the recipe, an italic serif font for the sidebar and a classy small font for the cooking tips. I have seen books with only one typeface that look very good. Italics or a different size of the same typeface can be used to give the sidebars or introductions a distinctive look.

Two keys to remember with fonts: (1) the font must be readable, and (2) all attention should be focused on the recipe itself and all other fonts on the page should seem less pronounced than the recipe and title font.

Try typesetting a recipe on your computer in simple serif fonts like Palatino or New Times Roman. Or try simple sans serif fonts like Arial or Universal. See how the page looks. It's very readable. That's the look you want to go for.

Calligraphy is another option. It's attractive for chapter headings or recipe titles. It adds a certain homeyness to a book, too. There are very readable cookbooks written entirely in calligraphy. "Handwritten" fonts usually do not grab attention like really good handwriting, but some come close. Find someone with excellent penmanship and have them write or print the recipes for your book. Poor, illegible penmanship will not work in a handwritten cookbook. Opt for a clean font instead. Some fonts that simulate handwriting seem artificial after reading a few pages, but you may find a classy one that will not get boring when used throughout the book. Try the "Calligraphy" or "Handwritten" versions of Lucida fonts or Corsiva fonts and see if they fit your needs. These fonts usually come with your wordprocessing software.

Laying Out Sidebars

Sidebars should look like something special. They need to be offset from the recipe. A background color for the sidebars that's only slightly darker than the page they're printed on works well. Frames are also good, but keep them simple. Desktop self-publishers have a tendency to opt for the most elaborate sidebars their publishing program has to offer. These will draw attention away from both the sidebar and the recipe.

The typeface of the sidebar should be either in a different size, in italics, or in a different font than the recipe. Using an italic version of the same typeface used in the recipe is almost always safe. Fonts that are two points smaller than the recipe fonts also look good. If you are using a different font, make it less obtrusive than the font used for the recipe.

Page Numbers

Page numbers should be usable. Put them on the top or bottom outer corner of the page where they can easily be seen. Putting the page numbers in the center at the top or bottom of the page makes the reader look harder to find them. I think the bottom outer corner looks best in the layout.

THE FRONT COVER

Front covers should be eye-catching. Even if you want a peaceful look to the cover, you must make it bold enough to be instantly readable. A light-and-dark contrast of letters and background works well, even if the light and dark are shades of the same color.

Cream paper stocks are elegant and warm looking. For my first book I used black letters on cream. For my second book I used cream letters on red. The title of your book should be easily read from ten feet away. You must grab the attention of someone walking by a store display. I used inch-high letters for the titles.

Covers should be simple. The title and your name are necessary, but use other elements sparingly. (I included a subtitle and a humorous illustration on one of my covers.) Simple line drawings are good. Color photos should be simple and grab the eye. Close-ups are one secret that food stylists use. Check out packaging of food products. You'll also see quite a few "enlarged to show texture" photos in food advertising. That's because a close-up of a slice of cake makes your mouth water, but a distant shot of a whole uncut cake may not.

Busy front covers are too confusing to the eye. Keep your cover simple and easy to read.

THE BACK COVER

The back cover is a billboard for your book. Use blurbs of praise for your book whenever possible. These are brief comments from readers, critics, news articles, etc. If you are home-publishing in small batches, you can revise your cover to add these recommendations once you've had some press.

The back cover is also a great place to get in a few of the key selling points of your book. What's good about your book? What's unique about it? Why would the reader want to buy it? Tell people on the back cover.

At the bottom of the back cover, make sure you put information about how to order your book. You should include the price and where to send the check. I can't stress this enough. I have sold hundreds more books by mail order because I put the ordering information on the back cover. Some people will copy it down in a bookstore and order later. Others will see the book at a friend's house and order from that. Whatever their method, you need to make it easy for them to order.

TITLING YOUR COOKBOOK

The most important words of your cookbook are in the title. These few words need to force the reader to pick up your book. The title must tell what the book is about and make the reader want to know more.

Titles should be one to seven words long. If you have a descriptive one word title, great. Titles longer than seven words get confusing. Starting with "The" and ending with "Cookbook" has always worked well. It's especially good if your book is innovative. *The Lithuanian Tamale Cookbook* says it all.

The further away you get from this basic success formula, the more you will depend on your subtitle. For instance *When a Lithuanian Gets Ahold of Corn* is a little obscure and long for a title. Instead try: *Lithuania*

Meets Corn with the subtitle *Meat, Vegetable, and Dessert Tamales With a European Flair.* That pretty much says what's inside.

Subtitles should be about ten words long max. It's important to remember that if people are tracking down a book with a search engine on the Web, your title and subtitle may be all they ever see of the book. So state what your book is about in the title or subtitle.

GETTING PEOPLE TO TAKE YOU SERIOUSLY

To make your self-published book an officially viable publication and more likely to be carried in stores, there are two things you need to have in it: An International Standard Book Number (ISBN) and a copyright notice.

The ISBN is vital for selling your book to stores or distributors. This is the book number used by publishers, booksellers and librarians for ordering and cataloging. You pay a one-time fee that gets you as many numbers as you need for as many different titles as you print. To get the form, contact the R.R. Bowker Company, 249 W. Seventeenth St., New York, NY 10011. These are the same people who put together *Books In Print*, so you might ask for the prices for listing in *Books In Print* while you are inquiring.

Listing in *Books In Print* will probably pay for itself in bookstore sales. Most full-service bookstores use this as a source for finding publishers.

The copyright notice protects your book and keeps someone from stealing your recipes and claiming they own them. The notice should appear in the front of the book. It's a "©" followed by the year the book was written and your name. Many people worry about filing their copyright notice with the Library of Congress before they print their book. Actually your work is copyrighted the moment it is created and you can notify the government once your work is done. You need Form TX from the Library of Congress, Washington, DC 20559. The cost is thirty dollars and you can send a printed copy of your book or the manuscript.

Who owns what? You own your book. You own the rights to all of your original recipes. If you sell your book to a publishing company, you are selling them your right to ownership. If you are self-publishing, you retain these rights free and clear. To protect yourself, anytime you send out a recipe or quote from your book, for publicity purposes etc., make sure you note "© (date), (your name) from the (name of book)."

It's best to copyright your book in your own name and not the name of your own publishing company. Some novice authors think this looks impressive and will grab attention. Actually it can be a legal nightmare. Let's say your copyright is not in your name but in the name of "Myvery-own Publishing Company." If your company were to get successful and you were to sell it, the copyright goes with the company. You no longer would have any rights to your own book nor could you claim any royalties.

Some chefs say there are no original recipes out there; that every one is a copy of a copy. For legal purposes, publishers will tell you, if three measurements are changed from the original, the recipe is considered new. That means if you just double the batch size of someone's recipe it can be considered your own because of the modifications you made. But honestly, it won't hurt your reputation as a cook to admit using someone else's original recipe. The recipe's author would probably be flattered to get her name in your cookbook. Ask permission, of course. And if the author admits that the prize recipe actually came from someone else, give both people credit. And it certainly wouldn't hurt to have a letter signed and dated by the author (or authors if necessary) that says that it's okay to use the recipe in a cookbook for the compensation of mentioning the author's name and maybe receiving a copy of your cookbook, if you can afford to be that generous.

Photography and Illustrations

Food is very visual. Any photos or illustrations you include in your book will enhance the mouthwatering factor.

Most self-published cookbook authors can't afford to have color photos printed by a commercial printer, but new color computer printers allow you to print reasonable-quality color pictures at home.

Classy-looking one-color line drawings of some of your food, or the raw ingredients, can also increase the mouthwatering factor. If a recipe is confusing, a line drawing illustrating the technique can be very useful to the reader. These drawings will reproduce well by all print methods. You might find a local artist or art student willing to work inexpensively or for a small cut of your book. Good-quality clip art is also readily available. Just make sure it is in public domain or copyright-free. Some clip art has the stipulation that if you are using it for profit, you must pay a royalty. Having experience in cartooning, I used humorous illustrations on the title page for each chapter of my books.

7 SELF-PUBLISHING

Printing your own cookbook can be a very expensive proposition. The first copy of your book can cost you hundreds to thousands of dollars to have printed, with each cookbook after that being very inexpensive. So it's best to print as many copies as you can afford to keep the costs down. The cost difference between printing 50 and 100 copies is huge. The cost difference between printing 5,000 and 6,000 copies is much smaller.

BINDING METHODS
There are many methods of printing cookbooks. Actually it's the binding method that will probably determine the quality and cost of your book. The following costs are based on printing 200 to 1,000 cookbooks, but can vary.

The Staple-Bound Cookbook
This is the simplest, cheapest, and fastest method of making a cookbook. It's usually printed on standard 8½″ × 11″ paper, folded in half, and then bound with two staples. The covers are usually a thicker Bristol or index paper stock. You can print it yourself on a laser printer or have it printed at a quick-print shop. Staple-bound cookbooks sell well at vacation spots, but bookstores are reluctant to carry them. Cost per book: $.50-$3.

The Three-Ring Binder Cookbook
Ring-bound cookbooks are preferred by some cooks because they lie open flat and they can add their own recipes. A local specialty printer (that prints on pens, hats, etc.) can print the cover on your binder at a reasonable cost. Another option is to print the cover on paper and use binders that have a clear plastic sleeve over the cover. Using the clear-sleeved covers costs much less than printing directly on a binder.

Half-size notebooks and paper work best, as full-size binders may not fit in some bookshelves. The pages for your notebook cookbook can be printed on a laser jet at home or by the quick-print shop. Cost per book: $1-$5.

The Comb-Bound Cookbook

Comb binding is standard for cookbooks and is inexpensive. The greatest advantage is that comb-bound books lie open flat for easy reading of recipes. The life expectancy is about that of a paperback, so many cooks prefer comb-bound cookbooks.

Most quick-print places can do their own comb binding. However, this is one of the most time-consuming aspects of printing. If you price the printing cost of the cookbook both bound and unbound, you will probably find quite a difference in cost. If you are going to print more than 500 cookbooks in your lifetime, it would be best to buy a comb binder for a few hundred dollars and bind the book yourself. You can get a commercial printer to print the title of your book on the comb, so it's easily seen on a bookstore shelf. Cost per book: $2-$6.

The Spiral-Bound Cookbook

Spiral-bound books are held together just like a spiral notebook. They use a plastic spiral coil that must be inserted by a commercial binder. If you have enough copies bound, the cost can be almost as low as comb binding. These books do not look as good as comb-bound, but they open more smoothly. They can lie flat open, and can also can be completely folded back. Cost per book: $3-$7

The Stitched or Glue-Bound Cookbook

This is the highest-quality and most expensive binding. It cannot be done at home. This binding holds up the best and looks the most professional. For keepsake cookbooks, a cloth or leather cover should be considered, but they are very expensive. Cost per book: $10-$25

Obviously people are willing to pay $15 for a beautiful cloth-bound book, but may not be willing to pay $8 for a staple-bound book.

If you're printing the cookbook for family gifts, you probably won't mind paying $10 or more to have each book printed. If your books are for a charity sale, a copy that costs a few dollars less than the sale price is not so bad. But if you're printing for commercial sales, the book cost must be 20 percent or less of retail. That figure may seem low, but for commercial sales there will be a lot of fingers in the pie recipes. Bookstores get a 40 percent discount. Distributors that sell to bookstores get a 50 percent discount or greater. Suddenly, you see you must keep your printing costs low to have any profit margin at all.

PRINTING YOUR COOKBOOK

Today the self-publisher has many options. Many printers cater to small runs of books. Some large quick-print places have copy machines that can actually spit out a completely finished book. The quality of printers for home computers is so good that for short runs you can do it all yourself.

Commercial Printers

I priced my first book at a hefty $14.95 and then sought a printer. I asked around and the best price I could find was $11.95 per book for 1,000 books. Later as book sales grew I went to a printer and paid $1.65 per book for 10,000 copies. As you can see, the more books you print, the drastically cheaper they are.

Price every commercial printer you have access to. Ask to see their work to determine the quality of layout, printing and binding. Find out if they've ever printed cookbooks before. Make sure your print job is not too small or too big for them.

There are numerous companies that specialize in printing small runs of cookbooks. The following companies are experienced in printing fundraising cookbooks as well as personal and commercial runs. The quality has been reported as good and they have a fast turnaround time. Ask for samples of their work. If you use one of these printers make sure you get only the services you need. While they are good for printing, you will probably do much better promoting your book yourself.

Morris Press
P.O. Box 1681
Kearney, NE 68848
cookbook@morriscookbooks.com

Cookbook Publishers Inc.
10800 Lakeview Ave.

P.O. Box 15920
Lexana, KS 66285
info@cookbookpublishers.com

G&R Publishing
507 Industrial St.
Waverly, IA 50677
gandr@gandrpub.com

It's a good idea to find a printer who can do a quick reprint order on your book. The price should be more reasonable and the turnaround time should be quicker, since they already have the elements together. Ask your printer what a second run will cost and how quick they can do it.

Printing It Yourself

I wanted 1,000 copies of my first cookbook printed. I discovered that I could buy the equipment and print it myself for half of what a printer wanted to charge me. I bought a used copier the size of a Yugo, a professional paper cutter, a laminator for the covers and a comb binder. It was a lot of work, but after printing and selling 400 copies of my book, I brought in enough money to pay for the equipment.

That included the $.25 it cost to laminate the covers. Laminated covers add a lot of value to a cookbook. Cooks will be willing to pay a few dollars more for your cookbook because the covers will last longer and they wipe clean easily.

Can you print books on a laser printer? The print quality is excellent and the pages will last, but laser printers are not designed to print 100,000 pages over a short period of time. You can wear one out quickly by running it constantly. The toner cartridges cost more per page than copiers do, and laser printers are very slow compared to copiers.

A used heavy-duty copier is a much better choice if you're producing books in quantity. Bubble-jet printers will not work for printing books. They use alcohol-based inks that smear when wet, and cooks constantly get cookbooks wet. However, you can use them for color covers that you laminate.

A good size to make a self-published cookbook is 5½″×8½″. These pages can easily be made by cutting a sheet of 8½″×11″ paper in half. There are a variety of paper and cover stocks available in this size.

FINANCING YOUR COOKBOOK

Finding the money to finance your self-published cookbook is the next step. If the book is for family, most likely your printing costs for 20 books will be $200-$500. This will probably come from your pocket.

The advantage of the charity cookbook is that you can presell copies and print the exact number of books needed. That way there's no financial risk involved.

As an entrepreneur you will most likely have to finance the venture yourself, as banks are reluctant to lend money to someone to print a cookbook. If you start a publishing company with the intention of selling your work as well as the work of others, and you have some manuscripts and promising projects to show, the bank may give you a small-business loan.

If you're financing the self-publishing of your own best-seller, it's good to have your own capital up front. Some people finance their book on a credit card. It's a gamble, however, as another 15 to 20 percent of the gross profits can be eaten up in interest in the first year.

PRICING YOUR COOKBOOK

If you have any intention of selling your book in bookstores or other retail establishments, you *must* use this pricing formula: Multiply the printing cost of your book by five. This is the minimum you can sell your book for. So if it costs $5 to print each book, it must have a retail price of $25. Bookstores take 40 percent, as will most other stores. With your cost at 20 percent that leaves only 40 percent for operating expenses and profit. You can see that if your book costs 30 percent or 40 percent of retail price to print, you can still lose money on each book you sell. If the formula retail price seems too much to charge, you probably are paying too much for printing and can't sell through most stores. You'll have to use a different sales method, such as mail order or person-to-person.

RELEASING YOUR COOKBOOK

I feel there are two good times of the year to release a cookbook. The first is in the fall. December holiday sales can account for up to 50 percent of annual sales. The drawback is that there is a lot of competition. More books in general are released in the fall than any other time of year. Another good time is February. Nobody releases books then and you stand a better chance of being noticed. In January, consumers pay off holiday bills, but by February they have money again. Some are already getting their tax refunds. If you release your book in February, you can do another push of your book in the fall and December of that same year.

A cookbook is a reasonably priced gift. Holiday specials can increase sales. Offer a discount for quantity gift-buying during the holidays. I offered a free calendar promoting my next book if two books were purchased for holiday gifts. Although 300 calendars cost me $600 to produce, and sending postcards to tell my customers about the deal cost almost $800, the cost was easily defrayed by the $8,000 brought in by the special.

DISTRIBUTING YOUR COOKBOOK

Once you have copies of your book, the next step is to get it to the public. If you have 25 copies and you're planning to distribute them as holiday presents, your entire distribution plan is just to gift wrap them. If they are for sale, then you need a better plan.

Fundraising cookbooks are usually sold to members of the organization selling the books. If yours is to benefit a group like this, encourage members to use them as gifts. You'll find many will buy more than one copy.

Your cookbook might also be of interest to people outside the group. Grocery stores, malls and other businesses may let you set up a booth for free. The best times are those that are heavily shopped. Saturday mornings are excellent. A lot of people also shop at grocery stores weeknights between four and six o'clock. If it's a double-coupon night as well, it can be a very profitable two hours.

Children in a group can sell fundraising books door-to-door. You think a door-to-door vacuum salesperson can be pushy. Just give a kid a stack of books and the prospect of making a dollar off of each one; the books will be gone in no time. Since the book is for charity, some people may feel the children should sell them with no compensation. You have to remember that kids are shrewd business people. If you force kids to sell books, you won't sell many. If you give kids a nice prize for each dozen books sold, you more than make up the cost in volume.

Local bookstores may want to carry the book. Of course they will want a cut. The standard is 40 percent, but since it is a nonprofit project, you may be able to talk them into 20 percent. If the charity has a Web page, put up the ordering information and you might get a few mail-order sales.

If you're selling a cookbook for profit, you will most likely be selling your book by mail order. There are companies who will do the order-taking, shipping and even the check-cashing for you, but until you are swamped with orders, you're better off doing it yourself. A post office box is not absolutely necessary, but it makes your business look a little more professional. Get the smallest box available to save money; after all you will mostly be receiving checks in small envelopes.

STORES

The next place you can sell your book is in stores. Grocery stores, cooking stores and bookstores are the likeliest places. Start with stores in your area. Call and ask who the cookbook buyer is. Ask if they're interested in selling your book and send them a copy. Tell them you're willing to do signings and cooking demonstrations. Expect to give a standard 40 percent discount to these stores. In some cases they will do a short discount of 20 percent, but if your book is for profit and you give them a more generous discount, they are likely to buy more copies.

To get your book into the national bookstore market, you'll have to sell to distributors. Book distributors are companies that stock for bookstores. They take a 50 percent or higher discount. The advantage is that they can get your books into stores that do not buy self-published books. Even if you only make a few dollars on a dozen books, it's best to sell to distributors if they want your title. After all, you wouldn't have made those sales otherwise. Tom and Marilyn Ross list a short, sweet selection of distributors in the back of *The Complete Guide to Self-Publishing*. They also give tips on dealing with distributors.

There are many other places you can sell books: school gift festivals, book fairs, farmer's markets and flower shops. Places that make gift baskets may also buy cookbooks. Cooking stores and cookbook store addresses from across the U.S. are available on the Web by doing a search for the word "cook" or "book" in Big Yellow at www.bigyellow.com.

MAILING OUT BOOKS

If you're mailing out books, the post office offers a special book rate. It's much cheaper than first class, but the book's time of arrival is unpredictable. It could take up to two weeks. Also, the rule is that you can't send personal messages with the book.

Priority mail is a service you should offer customers. It's not near as expensive as overnight delivery and guarantees two- to three-day service. Fast delivery for an extra $3.20 (weight limit, two pounds) is a good selling point.

People who do a large volume of mail-order sales sometimes use bulk mail. It is very cheap, but you have to do a hundred or so pieces at a time, and there are no guarantees with bulk mail. It's clearly stated that the post office has the right to destroy any piece of mail or bundle of mail that fails to meet requirements. And they don't have to notify you, so you won't know your mail hasn't been delivered until you have angry customers complaining they haven't received their books.

TAKING CREDIT CARD ORDERS

Taking orders on VISA, MasterCard and Discover cards will cost you a small percentage of the cover price of your book, but can generate income you might never get otherwise. Cookbooks can be an impulse buy, so taking credit cards at your book booth or over the phone can mean book orders that would otherwise be lost.

Shop around for credit card rates. Generally, a smaller bank is easier to deal with and has cheaper rates. You can even deal with a small out-of-town bank since most business is done electronically over phone lines. The drawback to smaller banks is that they get slower service from the credit card companies, since they're not big customers and are thus a lower priority for service and support.

The card scanner and printer you'll need can be bought or rented.

LIABILITY

With my *Fat-Free Junk Food Cookbook* I was concerned about diabetics endangering their health by eating a recipe with high sugar content. My insurance agent said the possibility of that happening was not the concern. He was more concerned that a baby could get hold of my book, eat a page and get sick from the ink. Surprisingly, he said, this is what liability suits are about. So the big concerns are not the legitimate ones but the lack-of-common-sense things. Liability insurance will protect you from both. Since you're not selling razor-blade balls or tasers, the cost of liability insurance is low and worthwhile for those selling cookbooks.

8 PROMOTING YOUR BOOK

Promoting your book simply means letting people know it exists. Start with your hometown and work your way out from there. And you don't need to be an outgoing, flamboyant huckster.

GETTING THE WORD OUT

Start by telling people you've written a cookbook. You'll be surprised how many books you will sell by just letting people know. Word of mouth is still the cheapest and best form of advertising. There's no need to force your friends and acquaintances to buy the book. Just tell them about it.

Most E-mail programs offer a signature that you can put on each piece of mail you send out. Mention "Author of the Blah Blah Cookbook" in the signature and you'll find people will start asking how they can get it. Keep a book or two with you at all times. People will buy books on the spot.

ALERTING THE MEDIA

The next step is to alert all the media on the planet. Why? The local TV or radio station may want to do a story on a hometown person who's successful. The food section of the newspaper may want to print an article on you and your book. You might become a novelty in another country and sell books ten thousand miles away.

The best source for media information is the *Gale Directory of Publications & Broadcast Media*, which is available at most large libraries. It lists every newspaper, magazine, radio station, TV station and cable outlet in the country. Entries are listed by city. *Ulrich's International Periodicals Directory* is a very thorough source of information on newspapers.

Who should you contact?

- Newspapers: the food editor or lifestyle editor

- Magazines: food and lifestyle editors
- Radio Stations: the news director, the talk show producer or specific show hosts
- TV Stations: the news assignment editor, talk show producer or show host

If you make a few calls and get the name of the contact person and not just a title, you are more likely to get a response. Also, you are likely to get a better response in your local area than elsewhere. So even if you are planning to become an international food celebrity, start at home. When you are ready to branch out, work to the next town closest to you.

Once you know whom to contact, send out media releases and try to set up interviews. Visit bookstores and let them know of any scheduled interviews: If you are getting publicity and are going to mention a bookstore where your book is available, they'll want it to be theirs. The largest independent bookstore in town will probably be easiest to work with and will pay you more quickly than the chains. Note that bookstores don't pay you for these appearances, so any money you make will be from your book sales.

People who listen to radio interviews are more likely to buy a book in a bookstore than by sending in a check or even calling an 800 number. Try to stock a local bookstore before a radio interview.

THE MEDIA RELEASE

Media releases used to be known as "press releases." They are still a very effective way to let the media know about your book. A solid release tells everything someone would want to know about the book and does it in one page. I have had articles and stories written straight from my media releases, so it's important to include all the details. The media wants to know who, what, why, where, when, and how much it costs.

Feel free to write your releases in the third person and tout yourself. After all, someone writing a story from your media release may use some of those juicy quotes.

A media release should include:

- **Contact Information:** Your name, address, phone, fax and E-mail. If you don't have access to a fax for receiving messages, you'll need to find someone who will let you have faxes sent to their machine. You may be able to make arrangements with your local library. If you're a good customer at the quick-print place, they may be willing to reduce or skip their hefty per-page charge.

- **Book Info:** The title, what the book is about, things that make it unique (writing style, the theme, who wrote the foreword), number of recipes, etc.
- **Author Info:** Your credentials. Why you felt there was a need for this cookbook. Maybe you feel there's not enough public health concern about diet, so you wrote the *Anti-Fat-Sugar-Protein-Cholesterol-Lactose-Free Cookbook*. Maybe you think there's too much concern for health so you wrote the *We're Gonna Die Anyway So Glut On The Good Stuff While You Can Cookbook*. If you write your media release in the third person, you can go ahead and quote yourself.
- **Any Recommendations About the Book:** Quote letters from readers, articles, interviews, etc. The more known the source is, the better.
- **Ordering Information About The Book:** The price, your P.O. box and/or your 800 number, whether or not you accept credit cards, and which ones.
- **Review Copies:** Note that a review copy is available on request.
- **Permission To Use Recipes:** Note that any three recipes may be used for articles, book reviews, or on radio and TV programs. This gives reporters doing a story or reviewing your book the right to use the recipes they want.

The Angle

Media releases benefit from having an angle to grab the reader's attention. What unique thing can you emphasize? If your book title is a real gripper, put it in big letters as a headline in your release.

You can do numerous media releases about your book. Many self-published authors send out a release every month. Tie your second media release into the time of year. What makes your book perfect for summer? Can it be tied in to Thanksgiving? Jane Trittipo, author of *The Marvelous Microwave,* got interviews near Thanksgiving from a media release about how to microwave a turkey.

Tie your book in with news events. If the president of the United States makes a comment about hot dogs and you wrote *The Hot Dog's Hot Dog Cookbook*, quote the president in big letters in your release and let the media know you're a hot dog authority.

I was surprised when a self-publisher told me that he had sent out his sixth media release on the same book and was still getting interviews. It's hard to believe that some people got five other releases and finally bit on a new angle.

Check Appendix II for a copy of a media release that was very effective for me.

PROMOTION TIPS

- Faxes are cheaper than mail and E-mail is cheaper than faxes. Use both to get the word to the media.
- Think of business cards as mini-billboards. They don't even need to contain your name and phone number, just a brief, enticing description of your book and ordering information. Stick them wherever you can. Hand them to whomever you meet. If you print the cards at home with a laser printer they can cost as little as $\frac{1}{5}$ of a cent each.
- After you have booked a radio or TV interview, send a list of "suggested" questions you'd like to be asked. It sounds pretentious, but it is becoming the norm in the understaffed media. The great thing about the list is that you are well-rehearsed on your answers since you wrote the questions. Also, send the receptionist a card with ordering information on it, since callers will be asking how to order.

PAID ADVERTISING

With all the free plugs you can get from the media, I'm reluctant to recommend buying advertising. Think about effectiveness: A one thousand dollar classified ad in a national magazine could better be spent on:
- phone time to fax over 4000 media media releases alerting them to your book
- 250 books and postage sent to key media contacts
- four years of Internet line time to put up a Web page and E-mail media releases about your book around the world

Classifieds, promotions and marketing activities are all a gamble, but promotions and marketing have much better odds. Media releases can lead to an article about your book. An article has a much better response rate than a tiny classified ad that few will see.

Beware of advertising specialists who seek you out. While some are reliable, far too many people have had bad experiences with people who call, write or E-mail them with shabby advertising opportunities.

If an advertising firm has piqued your interest, check them out and let them know you're checking them out before you agree to anything. Legitimate companies expect you to do this. If they have a bad track record or are scam artists, they won't call again.

- **Checking out advertising companies in general:** Call the Better Business Bureau and see if there are complaints about the company. Ask the company for customer references (which they should gleefully provide). If you try to call the references and get no responses, tell the company.

- **Checking out magazines and book-review publications:** If they're legit and claim to have been around for a while they'll be listed in the *Gale Directory of Publications & Broadcast Media* or *Ulrich's International Periodicals Directory*. Check their circulation numbers. If the ad costs more than a penny per reader, it's probably not worth it.

- **Checking out radio stations and cable TV stations:** They may offer to sell you commercials or even hour-long talk shows. No matter how appealing these can be, they're usually offered by small stations with few listeners or viewers.

- **Checking out companies offering advertising on the Internet:** These people are probably legit, but offer little for the money they charge. They can have the impact of writing your phone number on a public restroom wall.

THE PROMISE OF THE BIG INTERVIEW

Obviously, Leno, Letterman and Oprah are all interviews you want to do. But for the usual TV interview, if the station is not within driving distance and they won't pay for your plane ticket, you might want to turn it down. I know it's a big temptation to accept any interview, assuming you'll make up the expenses in sales.

Here's my sad story: I paid my own way to New York to do a morning show on a cable network. A limo picked me up at my hotel. The interview went great. I baked cinnamon rolls live on national cable TV. I sold two cookbooks off of it.

A few weeks later, I was a hundred miles from my home, in Lima, Ohio, and did a TV show that ran at 11:30 Sunday night. I sold 120 books off that interview. I discovered that the cable net had fewer viewers in the entire country than the local show did just in Lima.

A worthwhile place to advertise for interviews is *The Radio-TV Interview Report*. It's sent to every radio and TV talk show host and every newspaper in the country. For a fee, you can run an ad that touts you and your book to talk show hosts. The results are usually very good. I ran two ads and got forty-five radio interviews. Contact the publication at:

Bradley Communications
135 E. Plumstead Ave.
Lansdowne, PA 19050
(610) 259-1070

MAILING LISTS

Mailing lists are usually not a good buy for a small publisher. Many entrepreneurs who use mailing lists have told me that they consider a 1 percent return rate good. Simple math shows that postage alone will cost over twenty dollars just to send a postcard to one hundred people. Is twenty dollars per book sold (not including the cost of the mailing list) a good advertising buy? No.

MEDIA SAVVY

Being media savvy is a developed skill. Here are some tips:

• Don't talk about other radio or TV shows you've been on or other newspaper articles about you while doing an interview. Unless interviewers specifically ask how experienced you are, they probably aren't interested. Interviewers would hope that you are their "find" in their branch of the media.

It's okay to send newspaper articles to a radio or TV station or radio or TV quotes to a newspaper. Just don't mention the publicity you've received from a competing newspaper or station.

• Don't give just "yes" and "no" answers. Elaborate, but keep your answers brief. Two or three sentences at the most. In these days of sound bites, short, memorable answers are what interviewers are looking for.

• If you're going to interject humor, keep it short. Many times people don't want humor. If the host doesn't respond well to a joke or anecdote, get serious.

- On TV, look at the host when being interviewed. Ignore the camera.

COMPUTER MARKETING

Computers have not killed books as predicted. They have actually made them more popular. Amazon.com, the largest online bookstore, brought in $158 million last year. Online book marketing is still very inexpensive. Use it while it's cheap.

FREE E-MAIL

Juno offers free E-mail over most of America. It's a pretty good deal; you put up with their ads, you get free E-mail. Their software fits on a floppy disc, is easy to install and is available at www.juno.com. As of this writing, it only works on Windows 95 or later.

If you have access to the World Wide Web through any computer, including at the library, you can get a free Web mail account. Yahoo.com offers it as do many others. Type "web mail" into any Internet search engine and take your pick. Some tips

- By using the "Blind Carbon Copy" feature on most E-mail programs, you can send the same E-mail to a huge list of people at once, without their seeing all the other E-mail addresses you're sending it to. Mail the original to yourself and that way *Newsweek* isn't mad that they received mail for *Time* that was blind-carbon-copied to them.

- E-mail lists are a good bargain if you get them free. Mass E-mailing programs are available, but I shun both of these. There is still a lot of animosity towards junk mail on the Internet. If you send to the wrong person you may get a thousand copies of the same E-mail jamming your box or all your fax paper may mysteriously run out in the middle of the night.

- Any E-mail with the subject line written in all capital letters will automatically be deleted and not read. It's a sure sign of an ad.

USING THE INTERNET

To advertise on the Internet, you need a Web page. Most Internet services offer these free to users or for a few dollars a month. There are some easy-to-use programs like Hot Dog and Pagemaker that make putting up a Web page nearly as easy as typing and sending E-mail.

Remember that people on the net love free things. Once you have a Web page, offer a couple of free recipes. Change them once a month. Offer a service or information that is useful enough to keep people coming back to your page. Food history, a menu planner, cooking tips are just a few things that will make them return and tell others about your page.

Link your page to other pages. This is free advertising. Send E-mail to other cookbook and cooking-related pages asking to exchange links.

BOOKSTORE SIGNINGS

Presentation is important. People expect authors to be eccentric so it's okay to dress accordingly, provided you're clean and well-groomed. Make your samples and book display at signings as neat and orderly as possible. A nice tablecloth and a typeset sign telling what you're sampling will keep your presentation looking clean and professional. Always be on time for your signings and plan to stay late. If there's a crowd, it wouldn't be polite to leave. Sign whatever books you leave at the store.

Samples Sell

Whenever possible, give away samples at your book signings. Take advantage of places with hot ovens by baking things fresh. The aroma of freshly baked breads and pastry will attract customers. If there's no oven, microwave or refrigerator, bring samples that travel well. Serve samples on appropriately colored cocktail napkins or small paper plates.

Give out bite-size portions only. People are more likely to take samples if they can finish them in one bite. Make cookies small. And don't eat your own samples at signings. Mistress Manners would frown.

Always leave a few empty spaces on your tray. People are reluctant to take samples from a full tray because nobody wants to be first. It also makes people think your samples are in demand. It's OK to walk around the store and offer samples to shoppers. During the Christmas season, when checkout lines can be long, you have a captive audience. Bring over a plateful of samples and offer them to everyone in line. I've had numerous people leave their place to come over and get a book.

RELEASE PARTIES

Release parties are another way to sell your books. Release parties are kind of like "coming out" parties for authors. These gatherings are usually by invitation. The selected can meet you, buy your book and get it autographed. Not only do they get the word out that your book is available, these parties can also be big moneymakers. If your cookbook isn't written to benefit a charity, you might still use a worthy charity as a beneficiary and sponsor of the party. Your book is exposed to a market you might not normally reach, plus you're helping a good cause.

Contact the charity and tell them you'd be willing to do a signing-party fundraiser. Almost all charities are overjoyed when you offer them 20 to 40 percent of the party's sales. Some charities will give you the full price for your book and charge enough for party admission so they make money too.

A signing party benefits from an intimate location such as a large house belonging to a member. If there is enough interest, schedule two or more different sessions for the signing depending on the space available. You can also try a local posh restaurant. If they're normally closed on Mondays, for instance, they may be willing to let you have it then, provided their costs are covered. You can also hold your signing at a large hall or at your church, but it may lose some of its prestige. Since this is for a charity, your goal is to get the well-to-do there. They have the disposable income to donate.

With signing parties, you should make it clear that the charity will need to do the organization and incur the expenses of the event. You are donating your time and probably a hefty percentage of sales.

Make sure a charity has at least two months between scheduling and the event to promote it properly. Events thrown together at the last minute can have poor turnouts. Encourage the organizers to send invitations to members, their friends, local dignitaries, etc. Invitations with RSVP are the most effective way to get a good turnout. You might want to alert the media yourself, as many smaller organizations may not be well-connected.

Suggest that members make recipes from your cookbook as appetizers for the party. If you're holding your party at a restaurant they might be willing to cook your recipes for a reasonable fee, which should be covered by the charity.

Once you've done one of these events, you'll probably be contacted by other charities. You can do as many of these as you are offered and your schedule allows.

PRIVATE BOOK PARTIES

Mr. Tupper's sales method can work just as easily for cookbooks. Many women's groups, exercise classes and cooking groups meet regularly and are eager to have someone speak to them. There are also people willing to host book signing parties in their homes, just like those kitchen gadget parties. Offer them 40 percent of sales. They do the work and get people there; you show up, talk, demonstrate and sell books. Any group of a dozen or more works well. Less than a dozen in attendance usually doesn't bring in enough sales to justify your time.

SALES GIMMICKS

Though most of us would like to avoid them, they work. A packet of herbs or spices packaged with your cookbook can increase sales substantially. Include some bonus recipe cards with your book. Packaging a small kitchen gadget with your cookbook can work well too; for instance, a plastic garlic press with a garlic cookbook. Seed packets can help sell a fresh vegetable cookbook.

A book is a very marketable product. Don't limit yourself to bookstore and mail-order sales. Contact companies that create gift baskets, for example. A basket of fruit and cheese is an ideal place for a fruit or appetizer cookbook.

FREE RECIPES

Grocery stores are often willing to distribute free recipes. Produce markets, cooking stores, coffee stores, and craft shops are other possibilities. Ask the manager if they'd be willing to put out a stack of your free recipe cards. This also may encourage them to stock your book. Make sure you print book-ordering information at the bottom of each recipe.

DOOR-TO-DOOR FLYERS

Flyers are not traditionally the way to sell cookbooks, but the low cost makes this an appealing method of advertising. Flyers are about as effective as junk mail: if you get a 1 percent response, you're doing great. But the cost of getting them to your customers is much cheaper than junk mail.

If you deliver flyers yourself, you're only out the time and expense of printing them. Later, if the response rate is good, you may hire kids to deliver them for you. However, in the beginning, it's best to deliver them yourself to keep the cost down. The next time you take a walk, take a handful of flyers and tag them on the outside of the mailboxes you pass. (The postal service frowns on you putting them in the boxes.) If you place them beside the flag or on a nail on the box, they're more likely to be seen and less likely to be pitched with the junk mail.

The next time you're out of town, take some flyers with you. Send a stack to relatives and ask them to drop off a few when they go for a walk.

It's best to make your flyers about postcard size. Large sheets may not be opened and have a tendency to blow away. You can get four flyers from a sheet of letter-size paper or index stock and six flyers to a sheet of legal-size paper. This can bring your cost down to a cent or less per flyer.

MAKING THE MOST OF THE HOLIDAYS

December sales can account for a substantial portion of your yearly book sales. (Some holiday marketing strategies:)

- **In June, (when magazines are working on their Christmas issues):** Fax, mail, or E-mail magazines a note that suggests your book for any articles on Christmas-gift ideas. Include a brief synopsis of the book and a few reasons why it would make a good gift.

- **In September:** Get out your mailing list of people who've bought your book. Send them a flyer offering a quantity discount on two or more books or some sort of special bonus offer. Offer to autograph mail-order books for holiday giving, or mention that when they order a gift for someone, they will receive a free gift, perhaps a potholder, for themselves. Items with the title of your book printed on them can be cheap if you order them in quantity.

- **In late November:** Fax, mail or E-mail newspaper food editors suggesting your book as an item for holiday gift lists.

- **In November and December:** Find out where all holiday sales are, at schools, places of worship, homes and other locations in your area. (Check local newspapers.) Even if it's at the last minute, ask if they need another vendor. If they're not charging too much for booth space, sell your books there.

- Send a list of all your scheduled holiday book signings to local papers for their events calendar.

- Set up a booth next to a Christmas tree sales location on a busy thoroughfare. The landowner or tree lot people may not even ask for compensation, but make sure you get their permission. Also, check to see if you need a vendor's license.

- Those with no scruples may choose to send flyers about their books along with their season's greeting cards.

SUPPLEMENTING YOUR BOOK INCOME

There are few people who just write cookbooks for a living. The rare people who do put out a best-seller or two a year and work long hours at it.

The cookbook authors who are successful make most of their money from related side ventures. Marie Rama, who co-wrote *Cooking For Dummies*, spends most of her time as a spokesperson for Sunkist. Paul Prudhomme has numerous cookbooks, but his fortune comes from his prepared spice business. Many side projects will not pay much, but if you work full time at a lot of them you will find you can make it a career. Here are some ideas for supplementing your book income to make cookbook writing a more viable profession:

- **Teach a cooking class.** Apply as a teacher at all the local adult education classes you can find. Some grocery stores, cooking stores, and cooking departments at department stores pay you to teach cooking classes (and you'll also sell your book). Shaw Guides prints *The Guide to Cooking Schools*, a gold mine for those interested in teaching cooking classes around the country. When you know you're going to be in another city for a book signing or interview, you can use the guide to arrange a teaching assignment. (Note that you'll have to schedule these a long time in advance.) To get a catalog, inquire at:

Shaw Guides
P.O. Box 1295
New York, NY 10023
or at www.shawguides.com

- **Start your own mail-order catalog.** If you accumulate a mailing list from the books you sell, you will have a list of people who might want other things. What to sell? Aprons and mitts with your book title on them; homemade candies, cookies and snacks; kitchen gadgets that you find useful; bread mixes; your cookbook; other cookbooks, etc. (Check with the Post Office about any restrictions on sending food by mail, and with the Board of Health for rules on selling food by mail.)
- **Start a cooking newsletter.** Again, you've got your mailing list of your customers to start with. Newsletters can be made with a desktop publishing program and a laser printer. Once you've got 150 subscribers,

you can send it out by bulk mail and save on postage. It can also be sent out worldwide on the Internet with your newsletter as a cooking E-zine or by E-mail with no printing or mailing costs. Content? Print a recipe from your book in each issue. Offer cooking tips. An inexpensive way to interview famous authors is to find their names in your library's *Who's Who*, then send them a letter with your questions, leaving a space after each for the answers. (Make sure to include a self-addressed, stamped envelope for reply.) You can also interview by E-mail.

An easy way to get additional newsletter material is to have your readers write it for you. Put out a call in your first issue for reader recipes, anecdotes and book reviews. If you have a theme issue coming up, let the readers do the work; you'll find people happy to volunteer their opinions and knowledge. You can also sell advertising in your newsletter. Keep classified ads and quarter-page ad rates cheap and you're more likely to sell the space.

• **Write a weekly cooking column for the local paper.** These don't pay well, but book-ordering information will appear in each column and you'll turn into a local cooking authority. Your column may even be worth syndicating.

• **Become a speaker.** People who write books are for some reason considered instant experts. Churches and civic groups are always looking for speakers. Some engagements pay. Some groups will let you sell books and some will just let you pass out business cards. All appearances will spread the word about who you are and what you do.

• **Host your own cooking show.** Since you're an expert, offer your services to the program directors at your local talk radio station, TV station or cable outlet. Hosting a cooking show may or may not pay, but can really be career-boosting. You'll become recognized and your show will give you a place to announce your book signings, cooking classes, newsletter, etc. And there's no reason why you can't do radio *and* TV.

• **Start an in-home catering business.** Weddings, office parties and events are being held constantly. If you are handy at icing a cake and fixing food for a crowd, catering becomes an option as a side business. Some people just do cakes. Others specialize in catering functions. Or how about a Portable Party business where you deliver preplanned party packages. They're great for office and in-home parties.

• **Market your food products.** Nonperishable food items can be shipped anywhere. Perishable food items may also be lucrative. Some restaurants get their desserts this way. Check with the Board of Health for regulations first.

- **Become a rent-a-chef.** People are willing to pay for a chef or good cook to come into their home and fix a month's worth of freezeable meals for them.

Each of these sidelines helps to promote the other *and* helps to promote your cookbook. Many authors even drop the cookbooks when the sidelines get lucrative.

9 SELLING YOUR BOOK TO A PUBLISHER

I sold my first cookbook to the largest publisher in the country. But I was lucky; my book found its way to an editor's desk with a recommendation from someone else in the company.

After I had sold ten thousand copies myself, I got a call from the editor. I didn't think the offer was legitimate, since major publishers who you've never sent your book to usually don't call up out of the blue telling you they want to buy it.

Why the interest? I had the right book at the right time. I wrote the first fat-free cookbook on the market. I skipped the healthy stuff and went right for the fat-free junk food. It was an instant hit since there was no Snackwell's aisle in the grocery store then.

The contract took fifteen minutes to negotiate over six months. There were a lot of minute-long phone calls. We bargained and I got a reasonable deal.

I always assumed that an editor would be reluctant to take a self-published book. Actually, your success is looked at as a plus: If you sold two thousand copies yourself, they will assume they can sell a lot more.

After selling my book to the publisher, I went back and interviewed my editor. She talked candidly about what she looks for in a book. She also told me about proper etiquette in approaching editors. Here is what I learned.

THE QUERY LETTER

The first step in submitting your book to a publisher is the query letter. A query letter presents your book idea to an editor. In cooking terms, you're giving them a whiff. It should be straightforward and simple. Yours is probably the hundredth query letter an editor has read that morning.

Tell the editor in the following order:

- **What the book is all about:** Be thorough in twenty-five words or less.
- **Who the book will appeal to:** Who makes up the potential market for your book? Women? Men? Children? Young? Elderly? Married? Single? What income? What lifestyle? Eating habits? State briefly every possible group your book is marketable to, but never use the word "everybody." That's a dead giveaway that you have no idea who it appeals to.
- **Your writing credentials:** State any writing credits in three or four lines. If you have none, drop the paragraph. Don't apologize. Saying "I know I can be a great writer" will not sell your book.
- **If the book is self-published, state your success in real numbers:** How many books have you sold and how quickly did you to do it? Success is a big selling point.
- **Your connections with media:** State any interviews you've done or blurbs your book has received in magazines or newspapers. The truth is that the promotion departments in publishing companies are overworked and may do little to promote your book. The larger the company the *less* likely they are to promote it. Publishers are looking for people who are well-connected self-promoters.
- **Your connections with famous people who could do a back cover blurb:** Write to famous people and ask if they'd do a quick review of your manuscript. Many won't, but some are delighted with the attention. Is a friend's stepsister's second cousin thrice removed illegitimate aunt's ex-husband someone famous? Ask him to write a blurb for the back of your book.

That's it. The query letter should be one page maximum. Once your query is read and if the editor expresses interest, you go on to the book proposal.

THE BOOK PROPOSAL

The book proposal is an outline of the book and a few sample recipes or a sample chapter. In cooking terms, you're giving them a taste. Editors at this point would usually rather see proposals than full manuscripts.

Send them a complete list of recipes from the book. Mention that the recipes have been well tested. Send them a few of the best recipes from the book. Make sure each recipe is well-written and works; it might be tested by the publishing company. It is quite possible you could sign a book deal based on your proposal, before they have ever seen the manuscript.

THE MANUSCRIPT

If you've gotten past the proposal stage, the next step is to submit the manuscript: the entire chimichanga. Some publishers may want to see the whole manuscript before signing.

The manuscript should be printed with a 12-point, simple, readable font. It must be double-spaced.

TIPS FROM AN EDITOR

I asked my editor for some inside tips on what cookbook editors at the major publishing houses are looking for in cookbooks today.

- **Latest trends:** What food trend is hot right now? Better yet, what food trend will be hot in a year? Have evidence as to why the trend is growing: clip magazine and newspaper headlines, cut out TV listings of shows on the trend. Trends about to break or neglected existing niches are best.
- **Clever title:** My editor liked "The Joy of Soy" right off.
- **Catchy recipe names:** They should be mouthwatering and descriptive. They should be definitive and honest. "Best Italian Meatballs Ever" may be an instant turnoff.

ACTING AS YOUR OWN AGENT

I negotiated my first book deal myself. Blindly muddling my way through, I did pretty well, but here are some tips from my editor on how to negotiate:

- **Play it cool.** Publishing companies routinely sign deals with giddy, elated authors who give away the farm. Deal calmly and coolly with them: you'll get a better deal and you'll be respected more. It's like negotiating a deal for a car; you don't want to seem desperate.
- **Always remember that they want your book.** If you have something someone wants, you are in the driver's seat.

When negotiating:
- **Be fair.** Don't demand things just because that's what you've heard some other author got. Sometimes new authors negotiating their

own contracts get big heads, demand trifles, and then give away everything else that is important. Authors may demand signing tours that may do little to sell their book, and then give away valuable rights to get them.

- **Be honest.** If you are lucky enough to get more than one publisher interested in your book, let them know who you're talking to. Be polite if you start a bidding war.
- **Have a lawyer look the contract over.** A literary lawyer is of course best. If one is not available in your area, contact one anywhere in the country and work by fax or E-mail.

Once your book is sold, it's best not to become a thorn in your publisher's side. If they don't want to promote your book, for instance, there is very little you can do about it. The squeaky wheel doesn't get the grease, it just doesn't get phone calls returned. Complaining won't work with big publishers.

The easier you make a publisher's job the more they like you. Do everything you can to promote your own book. Ask your publicist what you can do to help make your book a success.

PERCENTAGES AND ADVANCES

Percentages are the amount you get from the list price of each book sold. Advances are money you get up front that counts against the royalty money earned by each book sold until the advance is made back.

You will probably get a deal between 5 and 9 percent, with seven percent the standard for new authors. However there is a trend with big publishers toward impulse-buy, short-life books. The idea is that the company prints a hundred thousand books and deep-discounts them to stores in an effort to get them on shelves for a nationwide sales blitz. The percentages are starting to shrink with 5 percent starting to become common in these deals. That means if a book sells for ten dollars, you get fifty cents off each book. Advances typically range from a few hundred dollars to ten thousand dollars for first-time authors.

There is controversy as to whether you should ask for a higher percentage or a bigger advance. Most professional authors go for a bigger advance. If your book is a million seller (as every author assumes it will be), you'd do better with a higher percentage. That's a gamble. What if for some reason your book isn't promoted by your publisher? What if it gets thrown into the remainder bins because of an executive pen stroke? It happens routinely through no fault of the author. Go for the best advance you can negotiate. High percentages are dreams. Advances are reality.

SELLING YOUR RIGHTS

Publishers buy rights to your book. You never sell all rights at once. You sell individual rights and get a royalty percentage for each of these. North American rights are the most valuable. Beyond that there are European rights, rights for other areas of the world, electronic rights, online rights, other media rights, etc. The more rights you sell, the more you should be compensated. To protect yourself, get a literary lawyer or literary agent when negotiating rights.

FINDING AND USING AN AGENT

An agent takes 10 to 15 percent. Good agents more than pay for themselves. They not only negotiate the contract, but they help you afterwards in dealing with the publisher; after all their salary is based on your book's success. If you have problems with your editor or publicist, ask your agent for help.

Agents are now as hard or even harder to land than publishers. Writer's Digest Books has a *Guide to Literary Agents*. Choose an agent carefully. Some agents charge reading fees. I'd avoid them. Some charge for expenses, like postage, phone calls, copying. Find an agent who deducts these expenses from the book's royalties. If an agent charges you anything up front, I'd steer clear.

There are many part-time agents. Some of these people send manuscripts to publishers indiscriminately and then charge the authors for it. It costs you less to submit your manuscript yourself and you'll probably get the same results they do. Plus they get 15 percent on the few they sell. Some of these agents are novices that have never even negotiated a contract. Find someone experienced who is really interested in your success. Ask an interested agent about their track record.

Look at the agent's listing in the *Guide to Literary Agents*. Does she represent a lot of clients? Did he sell a lot of books last year? The answer needs to be yes or you may be dealing with a novice agent or someone who wants payment up front, like the person yelling "pay first!" through a speaker at the gas station.

When I was negotiating the sale of my first cookbook to a publisher, my editor gave me a great "in" with literary agents. When you get to the point a publisher wants to buy your book, ask the editor you're dealing with to recommend an agent. Editors usually know reputable people they have a rapport with. That doesn't mean because those agents know the editor they'll get you a bad deal. After all, that would mean less money for them. You may find that an editor and agent who know each other will mean a smooth, easy relationship for everyone, including yourself.

RECOMMENDED BOOKS

The following books are valuable guides to cooking, techniques, food facts and self-publishing. No cookbook author's reference library should be without them.

ON COOKING

On Cooking: Techniques From Expert Chefs. Sarah R. Labensky and Alan M. Hause (Prentice Hall). A well-illustrated, easy-to-read book of classical cooking techniques. It's a crash course on becoming a make-believe French chef.

The Dictionary of American Food and Drink. John F. Mariani (Hearst Books). A comprehensive guide to why American food is called what it's called. It can make you an instant expert on food trivia.

A Gourmet's Guide: Food & Drink from A to Z. John Ayto (Oxford University Press). A dictionary of food terms and why we use them.

The New Food Lover's Companion. Sharon Tyler Herbst (Barron's). The most practical dictionary for cookbook authors. Techniques, prepared dishes, ingredients, etc., each covered in a paragraph.

ON THE TECHNICAL END OF FOOD

Kitchen Science. Howard Hillman (Houghton Mifflin). Tells all about chemical reactions in the kitchen and has a scientific explanation of how to make a perfect soufflé and why it works.

ON WRITING

Edit Yourself. Bruce Ross-Larson (Norton). An excellent book on clarity and word-fluff management.

How to Write Better in One Hour. George Mair (Stein and Day). Out of print as of this writing, this is quite honestly the simplest book on effective writing. It's worth the trip to the library or to a secondhand bookstore.

ON PUBLISHING

The Complete Guide to Self-Publishing. Tom and Marilyn Ross (Writer's Digest Books). The bible for self-publishers. Updated regularly since 1979.

EXAMPLES

THE ANATOMY OF A PRESS RELEASE

This press release worked well for me. It is one page long and tells almost everything the reader could want to know about the book. You'll notice that my credentials aren't listed. This release was for my first book; I decided to emphasize the uniqueness of the book since I had no cookbook track record.

Let's break it down and see why it worked.

IM PRESS RELEASE

IM PRESS[1]
P.O. Box 54172
Cincinnati, OH 45254-0172
fax (513) 474-2023

Interview Contact: Author[2]
J. Kevin Wolfe (513) 474-2022
(Leave message, call will be
returned promptly)

THE FAT-FREE JUNK FOOD COOKBOOK[3]

Recommended in the November issue of *Men's Health* magazine, the ultimate low-fat cooking guide is here![4]

Author J. Kevin Wolfe has removed the fat from the most sinful of foods. He's created recipes for brownies, cakes, snacks, and even oversized cinnamon rolls, all containing no fat, per FDA guidelines.[5]

"My goal was to keep the portions as generous as possible. At the same time I kept the flavor in the food. Many fat-free packaged snacks taste like stale cardboard. These fat-free recipes make treats that taste like the original."[6]

continued

These recipes include pizza, Crispix snacks, cookies, beer cheese, and even "intoxicating sherbets" made with liqueurs.[7]

The author has come up with some clever substitutions for fattening oil and butter in his recipes. In addition to the standard replacement, applesauce, he uses low-fat buttermilk, marshmallow creme, and arrowroot jelly.[8]

Wolfe's experimentation with fat-free junk food started with a diet in April last year. He lost 33 pounds in three months and has kept the weight off since.[9]

In addition to 100 fat-free recipes the cookbook[10] is loaded with informative and sometimes humorous sidebars. These notes deal with everything from coping with fat during the holidays to how to exercise properly to burn more fat.[11]

There are also numerous humorous illustrations by the author. The book is comb-bound so it lies open flat on the counter. The cover is laminated so it wipes clean.[12]

The book is written in a very practical style with one recipe per page so readers aren't confused as to which recipe they're reading. The ingredients are listed as needed in bold type. This eliminates having to constantly refer back to the ingredient list.[13]

The foreword is written by Lilias Folan. In addition to being a nationally respected yoga instructor and exercise consultant in the health field, Mrs. Folan is also the world's most followed yogi, thanks to her "Lilias, Yoga, and You" and "Lilias!" TV shows on PBS.[14]

A free review copy of the *Fat-Free Junk Food Cookbook* is available on request.[15]

Up to three recipes may be used in articles, in book reviews, or on cooking programs.[16]

Ordering Information: $14.95 postpaid to:[17]
"The Fat-Free Junk Food Cookbook"
P.O. Box 54172
Cincinnati, OH 45254-0172
VISA & MasterCard Orders:
1-800-DROP-FAT

1 I started my own one-person company to make the book seem more credible.

2 I put the contact information right at the top so the food editor or talk show producer didn't have to search for it on the page. I let them know they were contacting the author directly, which signaled that they could arrange an interview more quickly than if they had to go through a company press department. The "Leave message, call will be returned promptly" lets someone trying to contact me know that I would not be a wild goose to be chased. Some interviews you get because you are available at that moment, so let them know you're ready and waiting for them.

3 The title at the time was a clincher. There were no other fat-free books on the market and fat-free junk food seemed almost too good to be true and almost like an oxymoron. That got attention. The big bold title can't be missed.

4 A big magazine gave me a nice plug, so I heavily touted it. I did *not* send this release to competing men's magazines, obviously.

5 More baiting with some recipes for food that is delicious and normally dripping with fat.

6 Since the release is written in the third person, I took the liberty of quoting myself. At the time the few commercial fat-free products on the market *did* taste like stale cardboard. I wanted to let the media know that I had eaten the same stuff they had and was just as disappointed. Then I let them know that my mission was to come up with good stuff.

7 More recipe mentions. It makes the book seem packed with good recipes.

8 How did I do it? This is the type of thing that makes good article or interview fodder.

9 And what makes me such a big authority? I state the facts on my own weight loss which give more credibility to a low-fat diet.

10 If you've got a lot of recipes, tout them.

11 If you've got useful sidebars, let them know it.

12 The two best physical features of the book would be a plus if mentioned in an article or interview.

13 I felt this useful style was important. It's a draw especially to people who are new to cooking.

14 If someone famous has helped you out, let the media know. They may be saying, "Where have I heard that name?" Tell them.

15 Always let them know you'd be happy to send a book.

16 Give them clearance to use your recipes, so they don't have to call you. If they have to take any trouble, you could be skipped over for another story.

17 I know from experience that a newspaper will print your ordering information, so make sure they have it in the release.

POSTCARDS

Postcards can be used to notify both the media and the public about your book. They cost about a third less than a letter and are more likely to be read since they don't have to be opened up. This one announces a holiday special.

Give The Gift of Loss

The Fat-Free Junk Food Cookbook is an ideal gift for the weight-conscious on your holiday list. If you order before Thanksgiving, we have a special holiday offer. **Buy 2 Fat-Free Junk Food Cookbooks and receive a FREE Fat-Free Real Food Calendar** (normally $3.95) with a new fat-free recipe every month. You pay only $29.90 to get two books as gifts for friends or family and a FREE calendar for yourself. Isn't that clever of you? Send your check for $29.90 to:

The Fat-Free Junk Food Cookbook
P.O. Box 54172
Cincinnati, OH 45254-0172

Or if you'd like to order by phone with your VISA or MasterCard call **1-800-DROP-FAT.** Open 24 hours. Please get your order to us by November 24th to guarantee Christmas delivery.

INTERVIEW REQUEST FORMS

I find using this form is a quick and easy way to take down information on people who want to set up a phone or in-person interview about my book. Especially if you advertise in *Radio-TV Interview Report,* you will probably need it. Make the sheets small and leave a stack of them by the phone. Without the form, some of the information might not be taken down and you'll have to call back. That's time-consuming and costly for you and annoying for the caller.

Here's what you need to know:

- The name of the media and location if the interview is in person.
- What time the interview will be conducted. Check to see if they're in a different time zone.
- Who you will be interviewed by. Get the exact pronunciation of the person's name and the correct spelling.

INTERVIEW REQUEST

Where?

When?

Who?

Contact?

Phone?

Fax?

E-mail?

Receptionist?

Address?

- The name of the person who contacted you, if other than the editor, host, etc.
- The phone number of the contact person and a back-up number in case there are problems.
- Their fax and E-mail numbers so you can send them additional information and suggested questions.
- The name of the receptionist. This opens doors. Receptionists are the low person on the totem pole. If you call them by name and send a thank-you note, they really appreciate it. You should also fax or mail them your book-ordering information so they don't have to go fishing for it when callers ask about it.
- The media's mailing address for sending a review copy.

MEDIA ETIQUETTE

Generally the polite method of media contact is to send a book or press release. If you've sent a book, you might want to call two weeks later, just to ask if they've received it.

Not everyone you contact in the media will do an article on you or an interview with you. You will probably have a 1 to 10 percent success rate. That could mean that you send out 100 books and you get one interview. Those are lousy odds, but let's look at the numbers: For a $10 book, 100 books and postage might cost $350. If you're self-publishing and you sell 35 books by mail order off that one article, you break even. If you get two articles or four articles, you start turning a profit.

Some people have had great success cold-calling media contacts, stating who they are, and letting the person know they'll be sending a book. Remember, however, that editors, columnists, talent and producers are busy people, and if you have to leave messages, you will probably not get a lot of call-backs. A letter or E-mail stating who you are and that the book is on the way may be a better idea.

Always remember that you'll be much more successful with the media close to home. Get to know them, bake samples for them, whatever. If you make a splash locally, you stand the chance of your publicity shock-waving into the surrounding area and around the nation.

MEDIA CONNECTIONS

Though it's a lost cause, I've tried to be as current as possible with the listings for media connections. They were updated just prior to publication, but things change rapidly in the media.

E-ZINE CONNECTIONS

E-zines are World Wide Web newsletters and magazines. Viewership ranges from a few readers to thousands. E-zines appear, move and fold so rapidly that printing a list of them is useless.

The most up to date source is John Labovitz's impressive e-zine list. You'll find it at:

http://www.meer.net/~johnl

You can send E-zine editors everything by E-mail, including your book.

MAGAZINE AND NEWSLETTER CONNECTIONS

Here's a list of food, health and women's magazines.

American Health Magazine
Freddi Greenberg, Editor
fax: (212) 627-3833
28 West Twenty-third St.
New York, NY 10010
editor@americanhealth.com

Better Nutrition
James Gormely, Editor
5 Penn Plaza, 13th Floor
New York, NY 10001

Bon Appetit Magazine
William J. Garry, Editor In Chief

(213) 965-3600
fax: (213) 937-1206
6300 Wilshire Blvd.
Los Angeles, CA 90048

*The Cookbook Collector's
  Exchange*
Sue Erwin, Editor
P.O. Box 32369
San Jose, CA 95152-2369

Cooking Light Magazine
Mary Creel, Food Editor
(205) 877-6000

fax: (205) 877-6990
2100 Lakeshore Dr.
Birmingham, AL 35209
cookinglight@pathfinder.com

Eating Well Magazine
Marcelle Langon, Editor
(212) 767-6000
1633 Broadway
New York, NY 10019
ewelledit@aol.com

Family Circle Magazine
Nancy Clark, Deputy Editor
(212) 463-1000
fax: (212) 463-1595
110 Fifth Ave.
New York, NY 10011

Food and Wine Magazine
Nicholas Niles, Editor
(212) 382-5600
fax: (212) 764-2177
1120 Avenue of the Americas
New York, NY 10036

Food Arts Magazine
Michael Batterberry, Editor
(212) 684-4224
fax: (212) 684-5424
387 Park Ave. S., 8th Floor
New York, NY 10016

Good Housekeeping Magazine
Mildred Ying, Food Editor
(212) 649-3531
fax: (212) 581-7605
959 Eighth Ave.
New York, NY 10019

Harper's Bazaar Magazine
Annemarie Iverson, Beauty &
  Health Editor
(212) 949-3331
fax: (212) 262-7101
1700 Broadway
New York, NY 10019

Health Exchange
Brenda Hull, Editor
(303) 799-1683
104 Inverness Terrace E.
Englewood, CO 80112-5306

Health Magazine
Barbara Paulsen, Editor
(415) 248-2700
fax: (415) 512-9600
2 Embarcadero Center, Suite 600
San Francisco, CA 94111
editor@health.com

Health Perspective Magazine
Ruth Sirko, Editor
(314) 862-7800
fax: (314) 721-5171
8229 Maryland Ave.
St. Louis, MO 63105

The Hungry Mind Book Review
Margaret Todd Maitland,
  Managing Editor
(612) 699-0587
fax: (612) 699-0978
1648 Grand Ave,
St. Paul, MN 55105

Ladies' Home Journal
Myrna Blyth, Editor
(212) 557-6600

fax: (212) 455-1313
100 Park Ave.
New York, NY 10017
lhj@nyc.mdp.com

Let's Live Magazine
Beth Salmon, Editor
(213) 469-3901
fax: (213) 469-9597
444 N. Larchmont Blvd.
P.O. Box 74908
Los Angeles, CA 90004
letslive@earthlink.net

McCall's Magazine
Babs Chernetz, Food Editor
(212) 463-1451
fax: (212) 463-1269
110 Fifth Ave.
New York, NY 10011

Men's Health Magazine
Steve Slon, Managing Editor
(610) 967-5171
fax: (610) 967-7793
33 E. Minor St.
Emmaus, PA 18098

New York Times Book Review
Manuel Hoelterhoff, Book Editor
(212) 556-1234
fax: (212) 556-7088
229 W. Forty-third St.
New York, NY 10036

Newsweek
Richard M. Smith, Editor
(212) 445-4000
fax: (212) 445-5068

251 W. Fifty-seventh St.
New York, NY 10019

People
Nora McAniff, Editor
(212) 522-1212
Time Life Bldg.
1271 Avenue of Americas
New York, NY 10020

The Practical Gourmet
Gaylen Andrews, Editor
Gourmet Bldg., #102
Dept. NYO-92
7 Putter Lane
Middle Island, NY 11953-0102

Prevention Magazine
Mark Bricklin, Editor
(610) 967-5171
fax: (610) 967-7793
33 E. Minor St.
Emmaus, PA 18098
preventiondm@aol.com

Redbook Magazine
Dawn Raffel, Book Editor
(212) 649-3331
fax: (212) 581-7805
224 W. Fifty-seventh St., 6th
  Floor
New York, NY 10019

St. Raphael's Better Health
Magaly Olivero, Publishing
  Director
(203) 789-3972
fax: (203) 789-4053
1384 Chapel St.
New Haven, CT 06511

SELF Magazine
Rochelle Udell, Editor
(212) 880-8800
fax: (212) 880-8248
350 Madison Ave.
New York, NY 10017

TOPS News
Kathleen Davis, Editor
(414) 482-4620
P.O. Box 07360
Milwaukee, WI 53207

Vegetarian Journal
Debra Wasserman, Managing
  Editor
(410) 366-VEGE

fax: (410) 366-8804
P.O. Box 1463
Baltimore, MD 21203

Woman's Day Magazine
Elizabeth Alston, Food Editor
(212) 767-6418
fax: (212) 767-5602
1633 Broadway, 45th Floor
New York, NY 10019
WOMANSDAY@aol.com

Working Woman Magazine
Nancy F. Smith, Editor
(212) 445-6100
230 Park Ave., 7th Floor
New York, NY 10169
wwedit@womweb.com

NEWSPAPER CONNECTIONS

Food sections of newspapers tend to be the most receptive to cookbook news. A small paper affiliated with the Scripps-Howard or Knight-Ridder wire service may publish an article on your book and put it up on the wire. If it gets on the wire, it will be available to hundreds of newspapers.

Ulrich's International Periodicals Directory (in major libraries) lists newspapers and indicates which wire services they use. If you are notified by a newspaper that their story about you made their wire service, send out faxes, mail or E-mail to all the affiliates you can find. Let them know the article is on the wire and that you will be happy to answer questions or do whatever to help. I have made color photographs of some of my food available for free use by newspapers. Two of the wire services picked up articles about my book, *The Fat-Free Junk Food Cookbook*. Each article appeared in about thirty-five papers.

The Akron Beacon Journal
Jane Snow, Food Editor
(330) 996-3000
fax: (330) 376-9235
Box 640
44 East Exchange St.

Akron, OH 44309-0640
bjeditor@akron.infi.net

The Albany Times Union
James Gray, Food Editor
(518) 454-5694

fax: (518) 454-5514
Box 15000
News Plaza
Albany, NY 12212
tunewsroon@aol.com

The Albuquerque Journal
Susan Stiger, Food Editor
(505) 823-3926
fax: (505) 823-3369
7777 Jefferson, NE
Albuquerque, NM 87109
journal@abqjournal.com

The Arizona Republic
Patricia Meyers, Food Editor
(602) 271-8624
fax: (602) 271-8004
P.O. Box 85004
Phoenix, AZ 85004

The Arkansas Democrat-Gazette
Irene Wassell, Food Editor
(501) 378-3497
fax: (501) 372-3908
Capitol Ave & Scott St.
P.O. Box 2221
Little Rock, AR 72203

The Atlanta Constitution
Susan Puckett, Food Editor
(404) 526-5441
fax: (404) 526-5746
72 Marietta St. NW
Atlanta, GA 30303
constitution@ajc.com

The Austin American Statesman
Linda Wienandt, Food Editor
(512) 328-0180

fax: (512) 328-7304
P.O. Box 670
Austin, TX 78767
news@statesman.com

The Baltimore Sun
Karol Menzie, Food Editor
(410) 332-6156
fax: (410) 752-6049
501 N. Calvert St.
Baltimore, MD 21278-0001

The Baton Rouge Advocate
Tommy Simmons, Food Editor
(504) 383-1111
fax: (504) 388-0348
525 Lafayette St.
Baton Rouge, LA 70802-5494

The Birmingham News
Ginny MacDonald, Lifestyle
  Editor
(205) 325-2282
fax: (205) 325-2283
P.O. Box 2553
Birmingham, AL 35202-2553
70550.3405@compuserve.com

The Boston Globe
Gail Perrin, Food Editor
(617) 929-2802
fax: (617) 929-2813
135 Morrisey Blvd.
Boston, MA 02219

The Boston Herald
Jane Dornbusch, Food Editor
(617) 426-3000
fax: (617) 426-1315
P.O. Box 2096

105

Boston, MA 02106-2096

The Buffalo News
Janice Okun, Food Editor
(716) 849-4468
fax: (716) 849-3409
One News Plaza
P.O. Box 100
Buffalo, NY 14240

The Charleston Post & Courier
Connie Hawkins, Food Editor
(803) 577-7111
fax: (803) 723-4893
134 Columbus St.
Charleston, SC 29403

The Charlotte Observer
Nancy Brachey, Home/Garden
  Editor
(704) 358-5000
fax: (704) 358-5036
600 S. Tryon St.
P.O. Box 32188-28232
Charlotte, NC 28920

The Chicago Sun-Times
Beverly Bennett, Food Editor
(312) 321-3000
fax: (312) 321-3084
401 N. Wabash
Chicago, IL 60611

The Chicago Tribune
Carol Haddix, Food Editor
(312) 222-3232
435 N. Michigan Ave.
Chicago, IL 60611

The Christian Science Monitor
Marilyn Gardner, Women's
  Editor
(617) 450-2468
1 Norway St.
Boston, MA 02115

The Columbus Dispatch
Sue Dawson, Food Editor
(614) 461-5529
fax: (614) 621-0708
34 S. Third St.
Columbus, OH 43215
sdawson@dispatch.com

The Daily Oklahoman
Sharon Dowell, Food Editor
(405) 475-3304
fax: (405) 475-3970
9000 N. Broadway
Oklahoma City, OK 73114

The Dallas Morning News
Dotty Griffin, Food Editor
(214) 977-8417
fax: (214) 977-8638
508 Young St
Dallas, TX 75202

The Dayton Daily News
Ann Heller, Food Editor
(937) 225-2419
(937) 225-2489
45 S. Ludlow St.
Dayton, OH 45402

The Denver Post
Helen Dollaghan, Food Editor
(303) 820-1440
fax: (303) 820-1369

1560 Broadway
Denver, CO 80202

The Detroit Free Press
Patty LaNouns Stearns, Food
  Editor
(313) 222-5026
fax: (313) 222-5981
321 W. Lafayette
Detroit, MI 48231

The Detroit News
Robin Mather, Food Editor
(313) 222-2391
fax: (313) 222-2335
615 W. Lafayette
Detroit, MI 48226

The Flint Journal
Jennifer Kildee, Food Editor
(313) 766-6117
fax: (313) 767-7518
200 E. First St.
Flint, MI 48502

The Fort Worth Star-Telegram
Beverly Bundy, Food Editor
(817) 390-7421
fax: (817) 390-7831
400 W. Seventh St.
Fort Worth, TX 76102

The Fresno Bee
Madeline Davidson, Food Editor
(209) 441-6297
fax: (209) 441-6111
3425 N. First St., Suite 201
Fresno, CA 93726-6819

The Greensboro News & Record
Carla Bagley Food Editor

(919) 373-7057
200 E. Market St
P.O. Box 20848
Greensboro, NC 27401-2910

The Hackensack Record
Charles Monaghan, Food Editor
(201) 646-4000
fax: (201) 646-4135
150 River St.
Hackensack NJ 07601

The Hartford Courant
Linda Guica, Food Editor
(860) 241-6200
fax: (860) 520-3176
285 Broad St.
Hartford, CT 06115

The Honolulu Advertiser
Joan Clarke, Food Editor
(808) 525-8090
fax: (808) 525-8037
News Bldg.
605 Kapiolani Blvd.
Honolulu, HI 96813

The Honolulu Star-Bulletin
Cynthia Oi, Food Editor
(808) 525-8640
fax: (808) 523-8509
605 Kapiolani Blvd.
P.O. Box 3080
Honolulu, HI 96802

The Houston Chronicle
Ann Criswell, Food Editor
(713) 220-7373
fax: (713) 220-6806
801 Texas St.

Houston, TX 77002

hlfeat@lex.infi.net

The Houston Post
Janice Schindeler, Food Editor
(713) 840-6709
4747 S.W. Freeway
Houston, TX 77001

The Indianapolis Star
Donna Segal, Food Editor
fax: (317) 633-9423
307 N. Pennsylvania St.
Indianapolis, IN 46204

The Kansas City Star
John Martellaro, Food Editor
(816) 234-4395
fax: (816) 234-4267
1729 Grand Blvd.
Kansas City, MO 64108

The Knoxville News Sentinel
Louise Durman, Food Editor
(423) 523-3131
fax: (423) 673-3478
208 W. Church St.
Box 59038
Knoxville, TN 37950

The Las Vegas Review-Journal
Ken White, Food Editor
(702) 383-0211
1111 W. Bonanza
Las Vegas, NV 89106

The Lexington Herald-Leader
Sharon Thompson, Food Editor
(606) 231-3321
fax: (606) 231-3494
100 Midland Ave.
Lexington, KY 40508

The Long Beach Press Telegram
Elna Howe, Lifestyle Editor
(310) 435-1250
fax: (310) 437-7892
604 Pine Ave.
Long Beach, CA 90844
ptnews@ptconnect.infi.net

The Los Angeles Daily News
Natalie Haughton, Food Editor
(818) 713-3692
21221 Oxnard St.
Woodland Hills, CA 91367

The Los Angeles Times
Ruth Reichl, Food Editor
(213) 237-5000
fax: (213) 237-7910
Times Mirror Square
Los Angeles, CA 90053

The Louisville Courier Journal
Sarah Fritschner, Food Editor
(502) 582-4203
fax: (502) 582-4075
525 W. Broadway
Louisville, KY 40202

*The Memphis Commercial
  Appeal*
Christine Arpe Gang, Food Editor
(901) 529-2368
fax: (901) 529-5833
495 Union Ave.
Memphis, TN 38103

The Miami Herald
Felicia Gressette, Food Editor
(305) 376-3636

fax: (305) 376-2287
1 Herald Plaza
Miami, FL 33101

The Minneapolis Star Tribune
Ann Burckhardt, Food Editor
(612) 673-1726
fax: (612) 673-4359
425 Portland Ave.
Minneapolis, MN 55488

The Nashville Tennessean
Beverly Garrison, Food Editor
(615) 259-8333
fax: (615) 259-8820
1100 Broadway
Nashville, TN 37203

The New Haven Register
Carla Van Kampen, Food Editor
(203) 789-5200
fax: (203) 865-7894
Long Wharf
40 Sargent Dr.
New Haven, CT 06511

The New Orleans Times-
  Picayune
Dale Curry, Food Editor
(504) 586-3575
fax: (504) 826-3007
3800 Howard Ave.
New Orleans, LA 70140
webmaster@neworleans.net

The New York Daily News
Sally Han, Food Editor
(212) 210-2100
fax: (212) 210-2049
450 W. Thirty-third St.

New York, NY 10001

The New York Post
Jane Ellis Food Editor
(212) 815-8000
fax: (212) 732-4241
1211 Sixth Ave.
New York, NY 10036

The New York Times
Molly O'Neil, Food Editor
(212) 556-1234
229 W. Forty-third St.
New York, NY 10036

The Newark Star-Ledger
Ann Lerner, Food Editor
(201) 877-4141
fax: (201) 877-5845
Star Ledger Plaza
Newark, NJ 07101

Newsday
Irene Sax, Food Editor
(516) 454-2020
fax: (516) 454-2342
235 Pinelawn
Mellville, NY 11747-4250

The Omaha World Herald
Jane Palmer, Food Editor
(402) 444-1000
fax: (402) 345-0183
1334 Dodge St.
Omaha, NE 68102-1122

The Orange County Register
Joe Crea, Food Editor
(714) 953-2278
fax: (714) 543-3904
625 Grand Ave.

P.O. Box 11626
Santa Ana, CA 92711
ocregister@link.freedom.com

The Orlando Sentinel
Heather McPherson, Food Editor
fax: (407) 420-5042
633 N. Orange Ave.
Orlando, FL 32801

The Philadelphia Daily News
Deborah Licklider, Food Editor
(215) 854-5879
fax: 215-854-2391
400 N. Broad St.
Philadelphia, PA 19130

The Philadelphia Inquirer
Ken Bookman, Food Editor
(215) 854-5743
fax: (215) 854-4794
400 N. Broad St.
Philadelphia, PA 19130

The Pittsburgh Press
Suzanne Martinson, Food Editor
(412) 391-8208
fax: (412) 391-8006
34 Boulevard of the Allies
Box 566
Pittsburgh, PA 15230

The Portland Oregonian
Virginia Johnston, Food Editor
(503) 221-8599
fax: (503) 221-5306
1320 S.W. Broadway
Portland, OR 97201

The Providence Journal-Bulletin
Donna Lee, Food Editor

(401) 277-7847
fax: (401) 277-7461
75 Fountain St.
Providence, RI 02902-9985

The Richmond Times-Dispatch
Jann Malone, Food Editor
(804) 649-6820
fax: (804) 775-8059
333 E. Grace St.
P.O. Box 85333
Richmond, VA 23293

The Rocky Mountain News
Marty Meitus, Food Editor
(303) 892-5229
fax: (303) 892-5081
400 W. Colfax Ave.
Denver, CO 80204

The Sacramento Bee
Mike Dunn, Food Editor
(916) 321-1000
fax: (916) 321-1524
2100 Q St.
P.O. Box 15779
Sacramento, CA 95852

The Saint Louis Post-Dispatch
Barbara Hertenstein, Food Editor
(314) 340-7570
fax: (314) 340-3050
900 N. Tucker Blvd.
St. Louis, MO 63101

The Saint Paul Pioneer Press
Sue Campbell, Food Editor
(612) 222-5011
fax: (612) 228-5500
345 N. Cedar St.

St. Paul, MN 55101
scampbell@pioneerpress.com

The Saint Petersburg Times
Chris Sherman, Food Editor
(813) 893-8111
fax: (813) 893-8675
490 First Ave. S.
Box 1121
St. Petersburg, FL 33731

The Salt Lake City Tribune
Donna Lou Morgan, Food Editor
(801) 237-2045
fax: (801) 521-9418
143 S. Main St.
Salt Lake City, UT 84110

The San Antonio Express-News
Kristina Paledes, Entertainment
  Editor
(210) 225-7411
fax: (210) 225-8351
P.O. Box 2171
San Antonio, TX 78297-2171

The San Diego Union-Tribune
Maureen Clancy, Food Editor
(619) 293-1211
fax: (619) 293-1440
P.O. Box 191
San Diego, CA 92112-4106

The San Francisco Chronicle
Micheal Bauer, Food Editor
(415) 777-7044
fax: (415) 896-1107
901 Mission St.
San Francisco, CA 94119

The San Francisco Examiner
Jim Wood, Food Editor
(415) 777-7768
110 Fifth Ave
San Francisco, CA 94103

The San Jose Mercury News
Sam Gugino, Food Editor
(408) 920-5539
fax: (408) 288-8060
750 Ridder Park Dr.
San Jose, CA 95190

The Seattle Post-Intelligencer
Gregg Roberts, Food Editor
(206) 448-8356
fax: (206) 448-8166
101 Elliot Ave. W.
Seattle, WA 98119
editor@seattle-pi.com

The Seattle Times
Sharon Lane, Food Editor
(206) 464-2305
fax: (206) 464-2261
Fairvica North & John St.
P.O. Box 70
Seattle, WA 98111

*The Tacoma Morning News
  Tribune*
Don Ruiz, Food Editor
(206) 597-8742
fax: (206) 552-7092
P.O. Box 11000
Tacoma WA 98411

The Tampa Tribune
Bob Bowden, Food Editor
(813) 259-7617

fax: (813) 259-7676
202 S. Parker St.
P.O. Box 191
Tampa, FL 33606-2395

The Toledo Blade
Mary Alice Powell, Food Editor
(419) 245-6000
fax: (419) 245-6439
541 N. Superior St.
Toledo, OH 43660

The Toronto Daily Star
Marion Kane, Food Editor
(416) 869-4853
1 Yonge St., 5th Floor
Toronto, Ontario M5E IE6
  Canada

The Toronto Sun
Cynthia David, Food Editor
(416) 947-2222
fax: (416) 947-2441
333 King St. E.

Toronto, Ontario M5A 3X5
  Canada

The Tulsa World
Suzanne Holloway, Food Editor
(918) 581-8340
fax: (918) 581-8353
315 S. Boulder Ave.
P.O. Box 1770
Tulsa, OK 74102
tulsa@mail.webtek.com

USA Today
Linda Kauss, Food Editor
(703) 276-6532
fax: (914) 694-5018
1000 Wilson Blvd.
Arlington, VA 22234

The Wichita Eagle
Kathleen Kelly, Food Editor
(316) 268-6000
fax: (316) 268-6609
P.O. Box 820
Wichita, KS 67201

RADIO CONNECTIONS

There are a lot of cooking radio shows, but they can disappear quickly or move to a different station.

The Cooking Babe
Jayne Bonfietti
WDRC-AM 1360
(860) 243-1115
fax: (860) 286-8257
869 Blue Hills Ave.
Bloomfield, CT 06002
cooknbabe@adnc.com

Everybody's Cooking
J. Kevin Wolfe, Co-host
The X-Star Network
(513) 731-9898
P.O. Box 54172
Cincinnati, OH 45254-0172
jkevinwolfe@att.worldnet.net

Good Food
KCRW-FM
(310) 450-5183
fax: (310) 450-7172
1900 Pico Blvd.

Santa Monica, CA 90405

The Splendid Table
Lynne Rossetto Kasper
Public Radio International
table@pri.org

TELEVISION CONNECTIONS

Like radio, TV cooking shows come and go. It's also quite common that a cooking show you see on cable TV was taped five years ago and hasn't been taped since.

CBS This Morning
Beryl Kreisel, Book Producer
(212) 975-8118
fax: (212) 975-2115
524 W. Fifty-seventh St., Suite 44
New York, NY 10019

Food For Thought
Betsy Block
(904) 893-6666
fax: (904) 893-5193
WCTV
P.O. Box 3048
Tallahassee, FL 32315
wctv@edgenet.net

Good Morning America
Patty Neger, Book Producer
(212) 456-6157
fax: (212) 456-7290
147 Columbus Ave., 6th Floor
New York, NY 10023

Man In The Kitchen
Jeff Baker
Maninthekitchen@compuserve
.com

Monterey's Cookin' Pisto Style
Chef John Pisto
Monterey, CA
pisto@montereybay.com

The Oprah Winfrey Show
Guest Relations
Harpo Productions
110 N. Carpenter St.
Chicago, IL 60607-2101
(No need to call. The place is like
   Fort Knox. They won't even give
   out names.)

Regis & Kathy Lee
Michael Gellman, Producer
(212) 456-3045
7 Lincoln Sq.
New York, NY 10023

The Today Show
Andrea Smith, Book Editor
(212) 664-4371
fax: (212) 664-6345
NBC-TV
30 Rockefeller Plaza
New York, NY 10112-0002

113

The Tonight Show
Amy Gourwitz, Assistant
  Producer
(818) 848-2648
3000 W. Alameda
Burbank, CA 91523

Too Hot Tamales
Mary Sue Miliken and Sue
  Feniger
The Food Network

1445 Fourth St.
Santa Monica, CA 90401
mail@bordergrill.com

Vegetarian Country
Candice Masters and Molly
  Adams
(Syndicated on four California
  TV stations)
masranch@vegcountry.com

GLOSSARY OF PUBLISHING TERMS

Acknowledgment—The "Thanks to . . ." at the front of a book.

Acquisitions editor—The editor at a publishing company who buys manuscripts.

Advance—Money a publisher gives the author before publication of a book. Usually it's half on signing and half on delivery of a satisfactory manuscript. This money comes out of royalties when the book sells.

Appendix—The section at the back of a book where charts and additional information are placed.

Artwork—Anything graphic (such as illustrations or photographs), other than the text.

Back matter—Everything after the main text of the book, such as the appendix, glossary and index.

Back order—Order for a book that will be filled when the book is available.

Backlist—A term for books that are not new, but still available from the publisher.

Belt press—A printing press that also binds.

Bibliography—A list of books that were used in compiling a book.

Blurb—Copy that promotes a book.

Boldface—Bold type.

Bullets—black dots that highlight elements in a list.

Camera-ready copy—Art or text that is clean and ready to be shot with a camera.

Caps—Short for capital letters.

Case binding—Hardcover.

Chapter head—The chapter title.

Clip art—Generic artwork from a book or computer disc that can be used for publication. Usually this is licensed so the user pays no further royalty fee. Always check the fine print for the usage agreement to make sure.

Clipping service—A company that charges to keep track of articles on selected subjects in publications and clip them out for you.

COD—Cash On Delivery.

Collating—Putting sheets in the correct order.

Colophon—A description of production details (optional). May include the name of the typeface, printing process, etc., usually some unique details of the printing process worth mentioning.

Color separation—Acetate overlays of a work broken down into the four basic colors for printing.

Comb binding—Round-toothed book binding commonly used for

cookbooks. Its two biggest advantages are that it's inexpensive and the book lies open flat for easy recipe reading.

Condensed—A narrow version of a typeface.

Cooperative publishing—Of course they're cooperative; the publisher charges the author to print the book. About as effective as just hiring the services of a printer, but more expensive. They usually offer publicity services, but most authors find its cheaper and more effcient to do it themselves.

Copy—A book's text.

Copyediting—Editing for spelling, grammar, punctuation and readability.

Copyright—The right to sell and publish a book; a right that protects an author's work.

DBA—"Doing Business As."

Deadline—The date a work must be turned in to an editor.

Dedication—The published inscription at the front of a book.

Desktop publishing—Publishing done on a home computer and not in a print shop.

Dirty copy—Copy that is manually corrected to the point that it can't be read.

Dot-matrix printer—A computer printer of reasonable to excellent quality that prints tiny dots to form type and images.

Dummy—A group of pages that shows a rough layout of how the finished book will look.

Endpapers—The thicker pages next to a book's front and back cover.

Errata—Errors discovered in a printed book.

Excerpt—The literary equivalent of a sound bite.

Exclusive—A journalistic scoop.

Expert reading—A reading of your work by an authority on the subject to determine authenticity.

Fair use—The use of a small amount of material in a quote that is legal without getting formal permission.

First serial rights—Right sold to a periodical to print a series of portions of a book, usually before publication.

Flap copy—The fluff about author and book that appears on the inside flaps of the dust jacket.

Flat fee—A one-time fee for work done, with no royalties.

Font—A whole set of type.

Foreign Rights—Rights to a book sold to publishers in other countries. Usually includes rights to translate into a foreign language.

Foreword—Introduction to your book, usually by an expert.

Front matter—Everything at the front of a book up to the first page of actual book text.

Galleys—Can be page proofs from the typesetter or rough copies of your book from the publisher.

Glossary—A list of terms relevant to the work.

Graphics—Photos, paintings or drawings.

Halftone—A photo that has been scanned and converted to tiny black dots for easy reproduction.

In-House—Services that a publisher provides within its organization or facilities.

Inventory—Books currently in stock.

Invoice—A bill.

ISBN—International Standard Book

Number. A number assigned to a book for easy identification.

Jobber—A book distributor who resells books to bookstores.

Justified type—Type that is flush with the margins on both sides of the page.

Kill fee—Money a publisher pays for a writer's time when the work is not published.

Laser printer—A computer printer that is faster and sharper than a dot matrix printer. Can be used for printing small runs of books.

Layout—The arrangement of the elements on a book's page.

LCCN—Library of Congress Card Number. A number used by libraries for cataloging books.

Line art—A black-and-white line drawing.

List price—The full retail price of a book as listed on the cover.

Mail-fulfillment house—A company for hire that handles the process of filling mail orders.

Mock-up—A rough copy of a page, press release or promotional material.

Model release—A consent form used to get permission to use a photograph of a person.

Ms—Abbreviation for manuscript.

Multiple submissions—Offering work to more than one publisher at the same time.

Net receipts—Money a publisher takes in from a book's sale minus discounts and returned copies.

Off-register—Term that describes a color image with one or more colors slightly off center.

Offset printing—A print process that uses a flat print surface.

OOP—Out of print; no longer available from a publisher.

OOS—Out of stock. Temporarily out of an item.

OPM—Other people's money. Financial backing from others for a project.

Option—The right to sell certain rights, such as television rights. If your publisher has the TV option, they can sell those rights to whomever they want and the author is paid a percentage of the sale (as specified in their contract).

Ornament—Standard book graphic, like an enlarged letter to start a chapter, decorative line, tail piece or border.

Over the transom—Describes the submission of an unsolicited manuscript.

Overrun—Copies above and beyond an order of printed books.

Paper stock—The type of paper used for printing.

Paste-up—Finished copy with text and artwork, ready for printing.

Pen name—A pseudonym used by an author for writing anonymously.

Perfect binding—Glue-bound pages.

Plagiarism—Stealing someone else's work and claiming it's your own.

Point—Type measurement of $\frac{1}{72}$ of an inch.

PPI—Pages per inch. A measure of paper-stock thickness.

Preface—An author's opening remarks that tell why a book was written and what it's about.

Press kit—A package of promotional materials about a book and its author.

Proofs—Copies of pages for examination and correction of text.

Proposal—An outline and sample chapter of a book sent to a publisher to entice them to buy a project.

Public domain—Material not protected by a copyright.

Query letter—A one-page letter sent to a publisher to entice them to buy a book.

Recto—The right-hand page of a book.

Recto-verso—Printing on both sides of a page.

Reduction—Process of printing something smaller than its original size.

Remaindering—When a publisher sells copies of a slow-selling book to someone at a huge discount.

Returns—Books that have not been sold are sent back to the publisher by stores for a refund.

Review copy—A free copy of a book sent to a reviewer, an interviewer, or a distributor.

Revised edition—A new version of an old book with corrections, updated copy, or added material.

Royalties—Money paid to an author by the publisher for each copy of a book sold.

Saddle stitching—A center-stapled form of book binding.

Sans serif—Typefaces with no tails.

SASE—Self-addressed, stamped envelope.

Second serial rights—Magazine or newspaper rights to serialize your book after it's initially printed.

Short-rate discount—Any discount less than the traditional 40 percent.

Short run—A print run of a few hundred to a few thousand copies.

Sidebar—A short article or bit of information offset to the side, top or bottom of the page.

Simultaneous editions—Paperback and hardcover editions of a book published at the same time.

Slush pile—Unsolicited manuscripts sent to a publisher waiting for a junior editor to look them over.

Spiral binding—A plastic or metal spiral-notebook type binding.

Subsidiary rights—Rights other than book publishing rights included in contract, such as book club, paperback, etc.

Subsidy press—A publisher who charges to publish a book, usually little better than a printer in what they provide and usually more expensive.

Tearsheet—A clipped newspaper or magazine article, review or ad.

Tipped in—Term for an extra piece, such as a foldout that is glued into a book.

Title page—Page at the front of a book, giving the full title, the names of the author and publisher and any other information required by the contract.

Trade paperback—A larger paperback, up to 7″ × 10″.

Unit cost—The cost to publish each copy of a book.

Up charge—A charge over the expected price.

Verso—The left-hand page of a book.

Web press—A fast printing press that uses rolls of paper.

Work for hire—A work which the author is paid for but doesn't own.

119